# BATTLEFIELD
# WALKS
## THE MIDLANDS

*David Clark*

ALAN SUTTON

First published in the United Kingdom in 1993
Alan Sutton Publishing Limited
Phoenix Mill · Far Thrupp · Stroud · Gloucestershire

First published in the United States of America in 1993
Alan Sutton Publishing Inc.
83 Washington Street · Dover NH 03820

British Library Cataloguing in Publication Data
Clark, David
 Battlefield Walks: Midlands
 I. Title
 914.2404

 ISBN 0-7509-0285-2

Library of Congress Cataloging in Publication Data applied for

Typeset in 10/12 Plantin Light.
Typesetting and origination by
Alan Sutton Publishing Limited.
Printed in Great Britain by
Redwood Books, Wiltshire

# CONTENTS

# LIST OF ILLUSTRATIONS

# LIST OF MAPS

# INTRODUCTION

Walking is sometimes described as a 'skill' – mainly by serious walkers and enthusiasts, who occasionally present this pleasurable pastime as rather an exact science. Authors of textbooks on the subject regale the reader with stories of their most enjoyable walk, which is often too long and too harsh for an 'amateur' to undertake. None of the walks in this book would suit such hardened individuals.

All the major walks I describe are designed to be accomplished within half a day and allow time to appreciate and enjoy one's surroundings. They have the added advantage of being circular in nature – you always finish at your starting point – and take account of the walker's need for rest and refreshment.

Hopefully the walks will be of interest simply as walks, and certainly you should enjoy some splendid landscapes. However, you will benefit most from these battlefield walks if you also have some interest in history, which is a far from dry subject if a little fieldwork is introduced. By treading the ground once trodden by kings (and would-be kings) one can begin to experience more fully a sense of identity with the past – half-formed images of famous battles which have shaped our past and future spring to life as you stand on a hilltop or in a broad field where crowns were once won and lost.

Each walk concerns a battle which may or may not be well known, and is introduced with essential background information. Then follows an account of the battle, accompanied by a description of the results, backed up with some ideas for further exploration of the area in question, such as local museums and places of interest. In particular, the battlefield museums at Naseby, Edgehill, Bosworth and Worcester are excellent – though it is a pity that opening hours are often restricted to the summer months, thus necessitating a visit during a busy time. Finally, each chapter contains practical information, including the availability (or otherwise) of public transport, though detailed information on travel by public transport is often best obtained by reference, where possible, to the local tourist office, which is also, of course, a good source of information on local places of interest. Publicized opening hours are often at variance with actual opening hours, so it is usually advisable to telephone before visiting.

Whenever I go walking I take my 'flight-bag' with me, which contains the following items: camera, Ordnance Survey maps of the area, binoculars, pen and paper, compass, telescopic umbrella, cool drink (dehydration is a particularly easy complaint to acquire when walking) and a packet of biscuits (useful for diverting any unfriendly canine interest). I wear a shower-proof jacket, jeans and, most important, a pair of leather walking boots and woollen socks. (If you have room in your bag, a pair of ordinary shoes can come in useful, in the event of you wishing to enter a church, public house, etc.)

Some of the walks are easier than others, both distance and ground covered subject to variation. Most walks are muddy in parts, embracing low-lying land that was once bog or marsh. Even routes taking in roads involve some walking on often wet grass verges so do think carefully about footwear. (Incidentally, 'trainers' and the type of walking boots that look like trainers are very comfortable, but they are not waterproof and do not give adequate ankle support.)

The directions for each walk should be sufficiently detailed to ensure that you do not become lost. If you do, then the relevant Ordnance Survey map(s) should be useful. If you are not conversant with map reading techniques, a little self-study will soon enable you to find your way around a Pathfinder.

The key to a successful walk lies in adequate preparation. It is advisable to get acquainted with the route on paper before you start, and to leave yourself plenty of time to savour your surroundings. Completion time will, of course, be dependent on the individual, according to pace and requirements.

No introduction to a book of country walks would be complete without some reference to the 'Countryside Code'. Guard against risks of fire, take your litter home and do not disturb wildlife, plants and trees. Fasten all gates (whenever they can be opened) and keep to public footpaths and bridleways (when you can find them) across farmland. Similarly, use gates and stiles to cross fences, hedges and walls.

Do take care when walking on roads. Remember that you should be facing on-coming traffic, although sharp right-hand bends, the crests of hills and the lack of grass verges may necessitate breaking this rule. The important point to bear in mind is that you should always be visible to any approaching motorist. In this respect, country roads often require a little more care and attention than main roads. When walking in groups, stay in single file.

The walks featured are quite suitable either for groups of walkers, or for individuals to undertake alone, although it is always advisable to inform someone of your intended route and the timing involved. Unfortunately today it has to be said that women attempting any walk unaccompanied should take every precaution.

At the time of going to print, all the information contained herein is correct. However, the future of many famous battlefields is in doubt as sites fight their own battles for survival against developers. Also, the course of many of the battles cannot be described with accuracy, and experts must bear with me if I have sometimes generalized for the sake of clarity.

On the wall above my desk is a sheet of paper on which is written 'You can't please all of the people all of the time'. As far as the walks are concerned, however, this is just what I have tried to do. With everything from long country walks to short town walks, I hope there is a little something for everyone, and that the book itself will stimulate interest in battlefields and in the continuous fight necessary to preserve both the sites themselves and reasonable public access to them.

• Shrewsbury    Newark •     • Winceby

Stoke Field •

• Empingham

Bosworth •    • Polebrook

• Naseby

Worcester •
Evesham •     • Edgcote

Tewkesbury •   Edgehill •  Cropredy Bridge

• Chalgrove Field

**Battlefield Walks**
**The Midlands**

# INTRODUCTION

Within a few years of William the Conqueror's victory at Hastings in 1066, the feudal system became established in England. Feudalism operated within a fixed social structure. The land was owned by the monarch, William, who parcelled it out to his Norman followers in return for services – military or fiscal – rendered. These 'tenants', in turn, had the right to govern whomsoever worked the land and to levy their own taxes. There was no risk of one baron attaining a sufficient degree of power to defy the king because of the fragmented manner in which holdings were distributed. Indeed, rivalries and in-fighting within the baronial ranks ensured that the royal power base remained unchallenged. It was only through banding together to present a united front that the barons could hope to break the system. This they did, in a rebellion which resulted in the signing of Magna Carta at Runnymede in 1215. Fifty years later, a second revolt culminated in defeat on the battlefield of Evesham.

The only holdings with any geographical unity were those bordering Wales and Scotland. Although necessary to ensure that the Welsh and Scots were held in check, the risk to the crown became apparent with a further rebellion, destined to be brought to a bloody conclusion at Shrewsbury on 21 July 1403.

In order to survive, a medieval king had to be successful in war. If, as in the case of Richard II, he was unsuccessful, then he would be deposed. Of course, should he prove successful in prosecuting wars, then plunder would swell the royal coffers. But armies were expensive to recruit and to maintain. The best way to acquire the necessary funds was for a king to establish the right to tax everyone, and so to exploit the new commercial classes. Initially, the problem was approached by tackling *ad hoc* groups of merchants and barons and convincing them that it would be in their best interests to provide the necessary funds. The merchants, open to the argument that trade followed 'the flag', often needed little persuasion, while the barons, flattered by their monarch's appeal, usually followed suit.

In winning the support of both merchant and baron, a king would actually weaken his own position in what was essentially a demonstration of dependence upon his subjects. It was only a matter of time before such consultations became more structured and took on the guise of 'parliaments', a word derived from the French *parler* – 'to talk'. Eventually, the tables would be turned, with parliament controlling the monarchy, and a life and death struggle for supremacy between the two opposing factions. It is within this embryonic conflict that the internal strife afflicting Medieval England must be viewed.

# Warfare in Medieval Britain

Medieval European warfare was a slow, laborious process. An army which possesses the greater mobility is usually the superior force. Hence, in the thirteenth century, the Mongol hordes of Genghis Khan were able to sweep across eastern Europe almost unchallenged, the flower of European knighthood proving no match for the lightly armed nomadic horsemen of the eastern Steppes.

In Britain, the days of the heavily armed knight on horseback were numbered as early as the time of the Baronial Wars of 1264–7. The English longbow was already proving to be the terror of those against whom it might be employed. No matter how heavy the armour, a well-directed shot with the longbow could prove fatal. Therefore, the place of the knight on the field of battle was at the rear, behind both the archers, occupying the front rank, and the spear-men in the second. Uniformity was sadly lacking and the medieval army was all too often a rag-bag of poorly armed and equipped peasantry.

As far as tactics are concerned, one often gains the impression that medieval battles, like Saxon battles, were primitive affairs, little more than confused mêlées in which two opposing sides charged each other, head-on like rampaging bulls. And this was often the case with the archers, having shot their bolts, taking up pikes and cudgels and joining in. Such pitched-battles occurred because much of the weaponry available to the combatants was such that little damage could be inflicted at long-range. Pikes and swords were all short, while the battleaxe and mace, although requiring some space to swing, were designed to have the maximum effect at close quarters.

Strategies of commanders were often limited by factors outside their control. For example, troop movements were limited by the poor state of the roads. For military as well as everyday purposes, the only decent roads in Britain were the legacy of the Romans – Watling Street, Ermine Street and the Fosse Way, for example. Most other roads were little more than cart tracks, and this is why most of the major battles on English soil have taken place in the vicinity of the Roman roads. To steal a march on the enemy and take command of one of these vital arteries was the aim of every medieval strategist.

In addition to limitations of a geographical nature, prevailing social and political conditions also exercised a significant influence upon the conduct of campaigns. The fourteenth century witnessed a revolution in the waging of war, with the demise of traditionally 'feudal' armies and the growth of 'contract' armies. Instead of being expected to fulfil the obligation of serving his monarch for forty days each year, the knight paid a tax freeing him of this penance and enabling the king to hire mercenaries.

In one respect, the limited art of medieval warfare made a major contribution to the national heritage, for this was the age of the castle. Following the Norman invasion, castles were constructed in profusion throughout the British Isles. During the twelfth and thirteenth centuries, with military requirements in mind, they were developed and improved. Although, in the fourteenth century, the development of amenities began to take precedence over defensive requirements, they nevertheless retained a strategic and military significance for many generations to come.

# 1
# THE BATTLE OF EVESHAM
## 4 August 1265

## *The Road to Evesham*

In 1216 King John was succeeded by his eldest son, Henry III. It is said that John's death was hastened by the loss of his substantial personal fortune and jewels in quicksand as it was being transported across the Wash. The loss also meant that the new nine-year-old king had to be satisfied with a plain gold circlet at his coronation. John's reign had ended in civil war, brought about by his failure to adhere to the provisions of the Great Charter. Henry's accession led to peace and stability of government under the protectorship of Hubert de Burgh. Hubert, however, a firm believer in the concept of 'Splendid Isolation', fell from power in 1232, following an argument with Henry over a prospective punitive expedition to France. In fact, Henry developed into something of a Gallophile, surrounding himself with favourites from the Continent. In 1236 he married Eleanor of Provence, whose acquisitive relatives the king showered with gifts. Not surprisingly, the barons, supported by the Church, made efforts to curtail his income, with a view to limiting his liberality.

At the core of this conflict was the thinking that had gone on behind Magna Carta. Was the king to rule with absolute authority, or were his actions to be subject to baronial influence? Leadership of the opposition to Henry fell on Simon de Montfort, a brother-in-law of the king's through marriage to one of his younger sisters. Against a unified front of barons, clergy and merchants, Henry backed down and it was decided that, henceforth, the king should govern through a council to be elected by both royal and baronial interests. De Montfort, the driving force behind these reforms, was soon attempting to extend them to the autocratic rule of the barons themselves. However, while wishing to limit the despotic powers of the crown, the barons had no desire to see their own privileges eroded and the united baronial front began to show signs of weakening.

Henry and his son, Prince Edward, decided to take advantage of the growing unrest by dispensing with the services of the council's baronial representatives. Louis IX of France was brought in to arbitrate and not surprisingly came down heavily in favour of the monarchy. Civil war followed hard on the heels of Louis' deliberations. On the one side were ranged the king, together with the established baronetage; on the other were de Montfort, with his four sons, the younger barons and the poorer urban populations. Despite its deficiencies in combat experience, de Montfort's rebel army enjoyed his outstanding generalship and on 14 May 1264, at Lewes, the Royalists were defeated.

With both the king and his heir in captivity, de Montfort assumed the role of dictator. Like Cromwell after him, he was to discover that rudimentary steps towards democracy needed a firm guiding hand. Under de Montfort's short rule there were parliaments – occasions upon which representatives from the shires would meet to discuss the affairs of the kingdom – but at the same time, there were claims that de Montfort's supporters and, in particular, his sons were abusing their position in amassing considerable personal riches. Abroad, attempts were being made to raise a French army to come to Henry's aid, while at home there was fierce unrest in the Welsh Marches. Gilbert de Clare, Earl of Gloucester and one-time supporter of de Montfort, determined to take advantage of this unrest and began mustering his vassals on his Welsh estates in opposition to his former ally. As with many barons, he had grown resentful of de Montfort's unchallenged power and influence.

A further blow to de Montfort's plans came towards the end of May 1265, when Prince Edward escaped, fleeing to Worcester, where he assembled a Royalist army. In the latter part of July, de Montfort planned to march (with the captive King Henry) to Kenilworth, to join forces with his son, also Simon, who had been busily putting together an army of his own. Edward decided to prevent the link-up of the two armies by quickly moving in on Evesham himself. At this stage, the strength of the Royalist army was in the region of eight thousand men, while de Montfort, as yet unsupported by his son, could muster only about five thousand.

# *The Battle of Evesham*

On the evening of 3 August 1265, the rebel barons reached Evesham, where they rested for the night. De Montfort has often been criticized for his choice of camp site but, bounded on three sides, as it was, by the River Avon, the town might have appeared a defensively sound proposition. He could not have been expected to anticipate Edward's night march, which brought him to Evesham by the following morning. De Montfort's mistake lay in not keeping open the back door – the only bridge over the river at Bengeworth, on the present-day A44.

The rebels made a comparatively late start to the day. Henry, looking for opportunities to create delays, cunningly persuaded de Montfort to let him attend mass at Evesham Abbey. A rebel look-out posted in the Abbey tower had reported troops advancing on the town, but identification proved difficult as the Royalists carried rebel banners captured at Kenilworth. For all de Montfort knew, the newcomers could have been the Kenilworth contingent. By the time the situation became clear, Edward was on Greenhill and a cavalry detachment, under Roger Mortimer, held the bridge.

With the Royalists massed before him on the ridge, and Mortimer hovering menacingly in his rear, de Montfort took the decision to break out, choosing for his assault the weakest point, at the junction of the Royalist right and centre. Sandwiched between the cavalry and foot soldiers was King Henry, kitted out with rebel armour and a horse. If the rebel attack on Greenhill failed, the old king would be an early casualty, mistakenly cut down by his own army.

The rebel spearhead drove forward into the Royalist front line, which gave way under the pressure – but the rear lines held. De Montfort should have had the weight to break through, but at this crucial juncture in the contest, his Welsh contingent lost heart and retreated in disorder. Thus deprived of a large

An illustration taken from an English manuscript entitled 'La estoire de St Edward le roi',
c. 1255–60. It certainly depicts with accuracy the confusion of a medieval battle, and, in all
likelihood, the heat of the action as seen on the battlefield of Evesham (MS Ee. 3. 59, f. 32v. Syndics
of Cambridge University Library)

part of his army, de Montfort was lost. The Royalist flanks immediately closed in to embark on a slaughter of the remnants. Miraculously, Henry managed to escape serious injury, while all around him fell. With their horses gone, the rebel barons fought on foot until, overcome by sheer weight of numbers, they were cut down, one by one. While the battle raged, a thunderstorm broke out. According to tradition, when the storm was at its height and the battlefield in almost total darkness, Simon de Montfort fell.

Some two thousand five hundred rebels lost their lives, including Simon's son, Henry. Another son, Guy, survived, though frightfully wounded, somehow escaping the butchering of the rebel wounded by the Royalists that evening. The Welsh achieved nothing by attempting to escape. In their efforts to get across the river at Offenham, they were either drowned or killed by their pursuers. Even the deaths of the rebels were insufficient for the Royalists, however, who felt impelled to dismember the corpses. It is claimed that de Montfort's body, in particular, suffered special indignities, his head being sent to his wife – although Edward did allow the Franciscan monks to give such portions as remained a Christian burial.

Young Simon, who had answered his father's request for help too late, learned of the disaster while on the march from Kenilworth, and returned, a sadder and wiser man.

## The Aftermath

Following Evesham, Henry and Edward's priorities were to reward their supporters and punish the vanquished. The latter task was carried out with an enthusiasm which encouraged pockets of stubborn resistance to hold out for far longer than an alternative policy of appeasement would have rendered necessary. With Henry's blessing, his supporters freely pillaged rebel lands and possessions. Eleanor, despite being the king's sister, was forced into exile in France, and only her considerable resourcefulness enabled her to secure the safety of her remaining sons.

At length, Henry's repressive measures had to be tempered. For six months, Edward laid siege to Kenilworth Castle, which was held by rebels and proved impregnable. Another rebel band set up their headquarters on the Isle of Ely. While Henry and Edward were accordingly setting siege to Ely, Gilbert, Earl of Gloucester, appreciating the error of his ways, seized London. Henry and Edward, appreciating the error of *their* ways, climbed down and drew a belated halt to the reign of terror.

Edward became free to embark on a somewhat late crusade to the Holy Land, while his sanctimonious father was able to live out the remaining three years of his life in peace. He died in 1272, buried in his newly rebuilt Westminster Abbey.

Whereas Henry has been largely forgotten, despite his fifty-six year reign, the name of Simon de Montfort lives on, a symbol of hope for the oppressed. In his contemptuous dismissal of the de Montfort reforms, Henry seriously underestimated the strength of popular feeling running against the concept of absolutism, and he was forced to make concessions in order to restore a semblance of order to a country racked by civil strife. Although England was to continue to be ruled by the monarch, there was a tacit recognition that it should be governed in the interests of the nation.

At Evesham, the royal party had proved its point by force of arms and there would be no acceptance of the form of government prescribed by de Montfort. As this, in effect, amounted to pressure to sustain baronial influence, it might be argued that the nation suffered no great loss. However, the reforms Henry did choose to retain amply illustrate his guile and skill in dividing his enemies. Far from establishing their rights, the barons found that the rebellion led to considerable loss of prestige.

From the time of William the Conqueror, landlord and tenant had been locked into an immutable relationship, with the barons automatically exercising jurisdiction over the shire knights. This principle was abolished by Henry, who exempted free tenants from suit and service at a feudal court. Baronial powers were further eroded with the removal of the custom through which a baron would hear appeals from the courts of his tenants, all appeals being transferred to the royal courts. Thus the barons were deprived of both suitors and business. Although these changes were originally Montfortian, being prescribed during the period of the Provisional Government in 1259, it is worthy of note that Henry chose to retain them. In recognizing the rights of a stratum of society a layer lower than that which he sought to control, he placed a check on baronial ambitions – even if he failed to appreciate the true significance of his actions. Without the de Montfort rebellion, however, no measure of reform would have been possible.

# The Walk

**Distance:**    4 miles (6.5 km)

Begin at Evesham Tourist Office in Vine Street (point A). The building, originally an almshouse, also houses a museum (Pathfinder 1020 036437). As well as information about the conflict, the museum has a model depicting the battle. The almshouse lies within the abbey precincts, the abbey itself

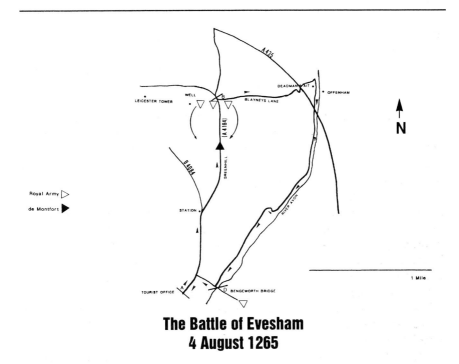

## The Battle of Evesham
## 4 August 1265

being founded in AD 700. It was destroyed after the Dissolution in 1540, and very little now remains. Two churches also share the precincts – St Lawrence's and All Saints. The bell tower, a late addition on the abbey's south side, bears musket shots made by Roundhead musketeers who used it for target practice. The famous stone monument to Simon de Montfort, standing about 50 yd to the south-east of the tower, was erected in 1965.

It has been remarked that a portion of de Montfort's dismembered remains were given a Christian burial by the monks of Evesham Abbey – a concession Henry was soon to regret when the tomb became a place of pilgrimage, where miraculous cures were wrought on the sick. The diseased part of the patient's body would be measured by a thread, which would be incorporated into a candle, as the wick, and lit. Another traditional form of healing revolved around the battlefield itself – earth taken from the supposed spot of Simon's death being sprinkled on a crippled limb. The 'Battle Well' also acquired a reputation as a spring with miraculous healing powers, the afflicted either drinking the water or applying it externally. An alarmed government did its best to discourage these practices, which subsequently suffered a marked decline in popularity.

Leaving the abbey precincts, walk back up Vine Street and straight on up the High Street towards the railway station. Just past the station, Greenhill begins. It was up this hill that de Montfort and his men marched to meet the

Royalist army. The area is a little difficult to negotiate now because it is so urbanized, but the rebel march was clearly not too onerous, the gradient being gradual and quite manageable.

The main action at Evesham took place to both the east and west of Greenhill (the A4184). To the east the land is fairly densely populated, and to the west quite thickly wooded. However, as one makes one's way up Greenhill, the occasional farm track leads off, between the houses, to the left. By following any of these tracks to the back of the houses lining the road, it is possible to obtain a fairly clear view of what is generally accepted to be the area where most of the fighting occurred. There is little to be gained by taking the B4084 Pershore road at the railway station and swinging round to the right at the junction with The Squires, for the roadside is thickly planted with trees and the view across country consequently much restricted. A landmark not readily visible at a distance for this reason is Leicester Tower (Pathfinder 1020 021367), built in 1842 as a monument to de Montfort, whom the Victorians saw as a patron of representative government.

Edward's position was at the top of Greenhill, where The Squires (the B4084) branches off to the left. The massed Royalist ranks must have presented a daunting sight to de Montfort, who knew his lines of retreat had been cut off.

In the belief that under such circumstances, the best form of defence was attack, de Montfort gave the order to charge. The momentum of the rebel assault caused the Royalist lines to give way. It was a desperate move that deserved to succeed, but, as the de Montfort spearhead drove itself home, the Royalist flanks turned in on the main body of rebels in a pincer movement. The only path of escape lay down Blaneys Lane (Pathfinder 1020 039456) (point B) to the right.

Walk down Blaneys Lane, now a single-track road. Now and then, there are gaps in the expensive houses lining the lane, providing a glimpse of a landscape which has changed little in seven centuries. Continue walking straight, down towards the new ring road (A435), which cuts across the path. Walk as far as it is possible to do and a diversion to the right, through the field, will become visible. With care, cross the road and make for the footpath sign by the iron gate on the other side.

Cross by the stile into the lane. Eventually the River Avon will become visible, with a wide expanse of grass opening up to the right, leading to the river bank. This is 'Dead Man's Ait' (point C), where many of the fleeing rebels – the Welsh in particular – were cut down by their pursuers while attempting to ford the river. Turning to walk back along the river bank, one can clearly see Offenham (Pathfinder 1020 053462) on the east bank, the road terminating abruptly by the inn.

Continue along the river bank. Fences have to be negotiated, but the going is good, considering the close proximity of the path to the river.

Looking towards Dead Man's Ait from the old road to Offenham Ferry. The River Avon is immediately behind the trees

Eventually, as one approaches Evesham, the path veers off to the right across the fields, and here the ground is quite boggy. Walk under the railway bridge and along the rough path, which soon develops into a single-track lane, leading into Common Lane, lined with terraced houses and, ultimately, into Mill Street, leading on to Bridge Street. To the left is 'Workman Bridge' (point D) crossing the Avon. At the time of the battle, this was the Bengeworth Bridge, beyond which Mortimer lay in wait should de Montfort have attempted to withdraw. By following Bridge Street and turning left into Vine Street, the Tourist Office and one's starting point can be regained.

## Further Explorations

The bridge now known as 'Workman Bridge' (named after a mayor of Evesham) is built on the original site of Bengeworth Bridge. Bengeworth itself has become incorporated into Evesham, but the castle belonging to the Earls of Warwick, which once stood by the bridge on the Bengeworth side, has disappeared. The B4035, leading eastwards from the bridge, leads to

Bretforton (Landranger 150 0943). The Fleece Inn, owned by the National Trust, can be found there. The fireplaces within have circles (known as 'witches marks') chalked on the hearthstones as a sort of talisman against witches entering the house through the chimneys, mirroring Worcestershire's reputation as a county with many associations with witchcraft and black magic – a strange contrast with the orthodox religious traditions as exemplified in its great abbeys.

# Further Information

Car-parking is not as difficult as one might imagine in Evesham, a popular base for touring the Cotswolds. Although short-term parking is plentiful, the walker will be looking for long-term facilities. I always use a car-park just outside the town centre, on Burford Road, off Port Street.

The railway station is on the London Paddington line and connections with Birmingham and the West Midlands can be made via Worcester. For details call (0452) 529501. National Express coaches serve Evesham via both the London–Worcester route and the Midlands–South West route (tel: 021 622 4373). Evesham has excellent facilities for the visitor although, along with many other areas, the town signposts provided for pedestrian tourists can be misleading. The Tourist Office, in Vine Street, can be contacted on (0386) 446944.

Landranger 150 and Pathfinder 1020 maps are relevant to this area. One of the best up-to-date accounts of the battle is *The Battle of Evesham* by D.C. Cox (Vale of Evesham Historical Society 1988) available from The Almonry Museum.

# 2
# THE BATTLE OF SHREWSBURY
## 21 July 1403

## *The Road to Shrewsbury*

The very first English Prince of Wales, the future Edward II, was appointed by his father, Edward I, in 1301. Not unnaturally, the Welsh took a dim view of this reminder of their subjugation to a foreign power. The last true Prince of Wales, Llewelyn ap Griffith, had been defeated by Edward in 1284, since which time Wales had owed allegiance to the English Crown. Huge tracts of the country were technically still the property of the Lords Marcher, whose claims had been staked at the time of the Norman Conquest but, for practical purposes, the Welsh were again under the jurisdiction of the king.

The imposition of an English 'Prince' did nothing to quell the almost continuous state of unrest in Wales. Neither did it prevent those with more coherent claims to the title attempting to prove their point by force of arms. Perhaps the most celebrated claimant was Owen Glendower, whose impressive pedigree included descent both from Welsh princes and Lords Marcher. In fact, there was much of the Royalist in Glendower's background. In 1385 he had assisted Richard II in his expedition against the Scots, and in 1399, when Richard was deposed by the future Henry IV, Glendower had given Henry his support. It seemed most unlikely, therefore, that he would be the man to assume leadership of the Welsh nationalist movement.

The rift between Glendower and the new king occurred when Henry commanded Glendower to accompany him on his own Scottish campaign. The order was channelled through Lord Grey of Ruthin, with whom Glendower had been carrying on a bloody feud over a parcel of land. It seems that Grey, keen to discredit his adversary, chose not to pass on the message, leaving Henry to presume that his order had been disobeyed. The end result was an armed rebellion by Glendower against the king, leading to the confiscation of Glendower's lands and a lasting and bitter enmity.

Signs of trouble were also beginning to appear further north, where Henry Percy, the 1st Earl of Northumberland, had been bearing the brunt of the continuous war against the Scots. According to the Percy accounts, a sum of some £60,000 had been expended in the process. Henry offered £40,000 in full settlement, which, in fairness, was probably all he could afford to pay. However, Percy and his fiery son, Sir Henry, better known as Hotspur, who had been instrumental in placing Henry on the throne, interpreted the offer as an expression of ingratitude and began plotting his overthrow. In fact, the Percys had always viewed Henry with some distrust. Their sponsorship of his cause had been limited to helping him regain his rights as heir to the Duchy of Lancaster. However, upon his return from the exile to which he had been banished by Richard II, he had proceeded to usurp the throne as well.

The Percy sponsorship was now bestowed on Edmund Mortimer, Earl of March and a descendant of Edward III, thus setting the scene for a dress-rehearsal of the Lancaster versus York confrontation. Sir Henry Percy had fought alongside Prince Henry in efforts to subdue Owen Glendower and he came to realize what a splendid ally this adversary would make.

The spark that was needed to set off the rebellion was provided when Hotspur captured the Scottish Earl of Douglas at the Battle of Homildon Hill on 14 September 1402. The king demanded that Douglas should be handed over to him, but Hotspur refused on the grounds that a healthy ransom for Douglas should help compensate him for the expenses of his Welsh campaign.

## The Battle of Shrewsbury

When ordered to return to Wales during the summer of 1403, Sir Henry Percy decided that it was time to act. His father, the Earl of Northumberland, took no active part in the insurrection, claiming to be ill. However, the Earl of Douglas was freed on condition that he should lend his support to the enterprise and so Sir Henry, together with his Scottish support, marched down to Stafford, where his army was further augmented by his uncle, the Earl of Worcester. From Stafford, the allies set out for Wales expecting, in transit, to meet up with Glendower.

King Henry had been in the process of marching north with a view to subduing the Scots, and at Burton upon Trent, he learned that he had been betrayed by Hotspur, his former ally. The timing was crucial. Had he continued north in ignorance, the situation might well have become hopeless. As it was, he wheeled about and made for Lichfield, where he was able to do some serious recruiting and garner further intelligence. Although he knew Hotspur was on the move, the king had no idea of his whereabouts and so, on 18 July, suitably reinforced, he marched north-west to Stafford. The following day, learning of Hotspur's plan to link-up with Glendower in the region of Shrewsbury, he embarked on a forced march to try to head him off. His anxiety was increased by the knowledge that the Prince of Wales, with a relatively small force, was at Shrewsbury, awaiting help. It was a close shave but Henry pipped the rebels at the post by a matter of hours. By the time Hotspur arrived, the town had already been secured against him. Glendower, he guessed, must be isolated on the other side of the Severn, and so, in an effort to find another place to cross the river, he retreated as far as the village of Berwick, where he made camp.

The morning of 21 July 1403 found Hotspur with his back to the wall. His projected offensive had been countered by the king's decisive march. The Prince of Wales was advancing towards him, while Henry, with the main Royalist force, moved out towards Harlescott. It was now Hotspur's turn for decisive action. Having been delayed by bad weather, Glendower was not coming, and it became imperative for the rebels to avoid being sandwiched between the prince and the king. Speedily vacating Berwick, therefore, Hotspur marched to Harlescott and beyond – coming to a halt to the north-east of the village, on a ridge running from east to west.

Detail from 'The Battle of Shrewsbury' from *The Pageant of the Birth, Life and Death of Richard Beauchamp, Earl of Warwick*. Hotspur's rebels are shown fleeing the field with the Royalist army (on the left) in pursuit (Trustees of the British Museum)

King Henry and the Prince of Wales, from their respective positions, followed, to draw up opposite.

Emerging from the town to try to effect a peaceful settlement between the two sides, the Abbot of Shrewsbury caused an albeit momentary pause in hostilities. Having failed in his mission, however, he withdrew, leaving the longbow men to commence battle. Initially, the rebels fared better, a well-aimed hail of arrows bearing down upon the advancing Royalists. The Prince of Wales was wounded in the face and the Royal bowmen's return was poor. Breaking ranks, they retreated into the Royalist foot divisions, carrying them along in their flight. Hotspur, who might have been better advised not to desert his strong defensive position, swept down from the ridge in pursuit. In the general confusion, he hoped to be able to fight his way through to the king. However, under Henry's leadership, the Royalists rallied and held their ground. The Prince of Wales, fighting on despite his wound, managed to break through the rebel right wing and so turn in on the main body.

The king had withdrawn to a position of safety but Hotspur, caught in the middle of the field of battle, fell, brought down by either an arrow or a spear thrust. In all likelihood, he suffered several wounds. Deprived of their leader, the rebels panicked, falling back in disarray. The Royalists took up the chase, pursuing and cutting down the rebels for a distance of over 3 miles.

## *The Aftermath*

Contemporary chroniclers considered the Battle of Shrewsbury to have been a particularly bloody affair, but it must be remembered that this was the first substantial engagement between Englishmen since Evesham, 138 years earlier. The significance of the encounter would have probably led observers to exaggerate the numbers involved. Henry's army, most likely around ten thousand, would have slightly outnumbered Hotspur's. Royalist dead would have been around two thousand, with rebel dead of perhaps twice that number, possibly up to five thousand, as a result of the merciless Royalist pursuit and the slaughter of the wounded on the field of battle by the local civilian population.

Hotspur's head decorated Micklegate Bar in York, and the Earl of Worcester's, London Bridge. While cruelty was the hallmark of the age, both York and Lancaster being guilty of their share, the Lancastrians tended to operate against a backcloth of carefully calculated piety. For sheer cunning, they could not be matched. It is said that Hotspur's assault upon the position of the king at Shrewsbury was doomed from the start because several knights, disguised in replicas of the royal armour, had been deployed to act as decoys.

A further story connected with the battle concerns Owen Glendower. Some say that he watched the whole battle from the top of a nearby oak tree – the implication being that he had purposely held back from joining up with his allies. It is difficult to see the advantage to be gained from withholding his support, particularly as he was later to enter into similar confederacies – again with the Earl of Northumberland who had somehow escaped the headsman's axe. Glendower may have used Henry's preoccupation with Hotspur as a smokescreen to extend his influence in South Wales but, in the long term, he could not hope to achieve any victory of substance without aid. Some support came from France, but it was going to prove insufficient to secure Glendower's aim of an independent Wales.

In 1405 Glendower, with the old Earl of Northumberland and Sir Edmund Mortimer, concluded the Tripartite Indenture, in which Glendower was to receive Wales, the Earl of Northumberland, the North and the Midlands, and Mortimer the remainder. Once again, however, Henry's timely action prevented a combined rebel force taking the field and although Glendower continued his border raids and maintained a façade of Welsh independence until 1409, his hopes of turning his aspirations into reality were at an end.

Shrewsbury deserves more attention as a battle that helped to shape the nation. Rebel success would have meant a weakened monarchy and a resurgence of baronial values. Instead, the young Prince of Wales was to prove his military worth, starting out on a road which, as Henry V, would take him to perhaps the most celebrated English victory of all time, at Agincourt.

As for Hotspur, he had to be content with his reputation – surely unwarranted – for rash impetuosity becoming absorbed into the English language:

> After him came spurring hard
> A gentleman, almost forspent with speed,
> That stopp'd by me to breathe his bloodied horse,
> He ask'd the way to Chester; and of him
> I did demand what news from Shrewsbury.
> He told me that rebellion had bad luck,
> And that young Harry Percy's spur was cold.
>
> Shakespeare's *Henry IV, Part II* (I. i.)

# *The Walk*

**Distance:** 3 miles (5 km)

Begin at the battlefield church on the northern outskirts of Shrewsbury (Pathfinder 869 513193), where parking is available. Booklets about the battle are available from the church, which also has a little reference literature and a model representing the action.

The church itself may be visited, and although Henry IV is often credited as the founder, it was Sir Richard Hussey, of Albright Hussey, who acquired the land for the founding of a chapel to commemorate the dead – between one and two thousand of whom lie buried beneath it. Suffering some damage at the hands of the Roundheads during the Civil War, the church almost became a ruin itself. Restoration work undertaken in Victorian times saved the day. When viewing the interior of a church, one always seems to look up, whether to view the roof, stained glass windows or memorials. However, in the present case, one's glance is directed downwards, towards the fine tiled floor – a home-grown product of Ironbridge. Fastened to the hammerbeams are the coats-of-arms of the knights who fought in the battle. These include the arms of the Earl of Stafford, Sir Walter Blount and Sir Richard Hussey.

Leaving the church (point A), turn to the left, and go through the churchyard to the wooden stile (in poor repair). Climb over with care and follow the hedge on the right.

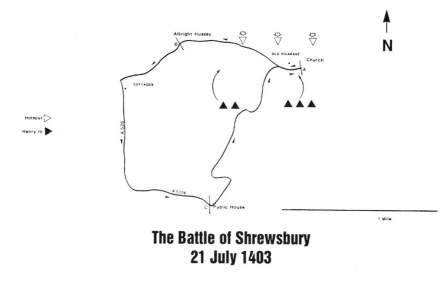

**The Battle of Shrewsbury
21 July 1403**

Hotspur's rebels occupied a position to the rear of the church and vicarage, the Royalist army advancing towards them from the foreground of this picture

The landscape has changed much in the past twenty years. For example, the vicarage, on the right, is now a private residence, known as The Field House. It appears to have acquired much land, presently hedged off, which was once pasture. Hotspur's position was beyond the church, Henry's directly in front of it. The marshy area by the stile leading into the churchyard may have developed from the cellars and foundations of the chantry, established shortly after the church, which fell into disrepair at the Dissolution of the Monasteries.

Continue to follow the hedge until arrival at a copse, through which a path for farm vehicles has been cleared. Keep on, through to the next field – a long field which broadens out towards the end. At a point not very far removed from the copse, the Prince of Wales swept across to attack Hotspur's right wing. A glance to the left shows that the Royalists were having to advance uphill in order to mount their assault on Hotspur's well-chosen position.

Walking through into the next field, the path (depicted on Pathfinder 839 504163 as a bridle-path, though ill-defined) widens out into a farm track. Ahead is a group of buildings which, at a distance and from the direction of approach, resembles an industrial site. Bear left and a single-track road leading down to the A528 becomes visible. As one approaches the front of the buildings, they become more identifiable as the Albright Hussey estate (point B), a half-timbered sixteenth-century house with outbuildings, now a prestigious hotel and restaurant – most definitely not a port of call for ramblers. During the later Civil War, the estate was used as a Royalist garrison to cover Roundhead-occupied Wem, to the north.

Turn left on to the A528. Just before the line of electricity pylons (also good landmarks) there was originally a footpath off to the left. Since this has now been removed, the A528 must be followed (with care) down to the next road junction on the left, with Harlescott Road (the A5124). Turn into Harlescott Road, where a wide grass verge on the left makes for easier walking. A second public footpath (which should branch off towards the church) has been blocked by a new industrial estate – but do not despair! Walk on towards the older industrial estate in the middle distance. A new pub, the Harry Hotspur (point C) on the right, constitutes an opportunity for refreshment.

Take the road directly opposite the pub, which leads down the side of the old industrial estate, and terminates beyond a 'Farm Vehicles Only' sign. In front of the farm-workers' cottages, turn sharp left and climb the gate, to follow a cinder track. At the end of the track, turn sharp right and climb another gate – picking up with the public footpath, which used to lead directly from the road. Keep straight on, towards a line of pylons. Negotiate a third gate and walk beneath the pylons, following the hedgerow round to the right, and then sharply to the left. The church will come into view. On turning this corner, scramble through to the field on the left and continue to follow the hedgerow. Keep straight ahead to arrive back at the clearing in the copse. The path (to the right) back to the church is now clear.

Walkers will be interested to learn that at the time of writing (Spring 1993) a new public footpath system in proximity to the battlefield is being planned by Shropshire County Council.

# Further Explorations

The battlefield covers a small area and the walk is necessarily a short one, so visitors can allow time to visit Shrewsbury itself. Shrewsbury Castle (Pathfinder 869 495129) is of Norman origin, although damage inflicted upon it by Welsh raids led to it being rebuilt in the fourteenth century. During the Civil War, Prince Rupert, as Royalist Commander of Wales and the Marches, established his headquarters here. In 1645 the garrison surrendered to the Roundheads, the castle surviving to be converted into a house in the eighteenth century. In a half-timbered house on the quaintly named Wyle Cop, Henry VII is said to have lodged en route to Bosworth.

To the east of the town is a wooded area called Haughmond Hill (Landranger 126 5413). According to local tradition, it was named accidentally by Henry IV's queen, Joanna, who allegedly watched the progress of the battle from that point. When it was all over, breathing a sigh of relief, she said 'Amen'. From that time, the spot was referred to as 'Amen Hill' which, in time, developed into 'Haughmond Hill'. Sheltered beneath the hill is Haughmond Abbey, a twelfth-century Augustinian priory. It suffered damage during the Dissolution, the remains being converted into a house. This, in turn, was burned down during the Civil War. The ruins are open to the public.

Eaton Constantine (Landranger 126 5906) has a timber-framed building (marked on the map) called Baxter's House. Richard Baxter, who spent his childhood here, was Chaplain to Col. Barker, Governor of Coventry, and then Col. Whalley's regiment in the New Model Army during the Civil War, although he became unpopular by his opposition to the execution of the king. After the Restoration he was imprisoned for his revolutionary views – succeeding in antagonizing both camps by his moderation. Baxter's writings on events in the Civil War constitute valuable source material.

A little further west is a landmark which visitors cannot have failed to notice – The Wrekin (Landranger 127 6208), an isolated hill rising from the Severn Plain. An Iron Age fort crowns the 1,334 ft high summit. A stronghold of the Cornovii people – one of the last tribes to hold out against the Romans – it was formed, according to legend, by a giant who dropped a load of earth he was moving to dam the River Severn and flood Shrewsbury. As all true Cockneys are born within the sound of Bow Bells, so all true Salopians are born within sight of The Wrekin.

On the eastern fringes of Shropshire is Boscobel House (Landranger 127 8308) where the future Charles II stayed after the Battle of Worcester (see p. 150). Although the famous oak tree no longer exists, it is believed that the tree currently occupying the spot is a direct descendant.

Shropshire has suffered, perhaps even more than most counties, from many internal wars. Favourite raiding country for the Welsh, Glendower did much damage in the fourteenth century. Although relatively unscathed by the Wars of the Roses, many fine houses and estates were laid waste by the Roundheads during the Civil War. Having said this, some splendid Elizabethan mansions have survived, notably Pitchford Hall (Landranger 126 5204), a magnificent black and white timber-framed building, and the nearby Condover Hall (Landranger 126 4905), built of stone. The latter, now a school for the blind, may be visited by appointment (tel: 074 372 2320).

# Further Information

Shrewsbury is situated on the A5 between Oswestry and Telford. The town is quite accessible, thanks to the M6 and, in particular, the M54 and the new ring road, which leads almost directly to the battlefield itself – to the north of the town, off the A49 Whitchurch Road. A single-track road leads under an old railway bridge to the church, which can be seen from the main road. A sign indicating the turn-off is usually placed there when the church is open (Sundays 2–5 pm, 1 May–31 August).

The town has a busy railway station, from which lines radiate in four directions. Telephone Shrewsbury (0743) 364041 for details of services. For details of National Express coach services to the area call 021 622 4373. As the battlefield is 3 miles from the town centre, local bus services assume some importance. For details of services between Shrewsbury and the locality of the battle site contact the Tourist Office on (0743) 350761.

Ordnance Survey maps Landranger 126 and 127 and Pathfinder 869 refer, while a useful chapter on the battle can be found in A.H. Burne's *Battlefields of England* (Methuen 1950) and Philip Warner's *British Battlefields: The South* (Osprey 1972). A booklet, *The Battle of Shrewsbury* by E.J. Priestley, is available from Clive House Museum, College Hill, Shrewsbury.

# INTRODUCTION

One may be forgiven for considering the history of the Wars of the Roses as a very complicated affair. The rivalry between the Houses of York and Lancaster lasted for a century and it is certainly difficult to present a brief overview of events. The time span involved, in association with the brief life expectancy of the times, means that many people share the same title. The period saw five Earls of Suffolk, four Dukes of York, five Earls of Pembroke and sundry earls, dukes and marquis of Somerset. To further confuse the issue, several of the major protagonists kept changing sides.

The death of Edward III in 1377 marked the end of fifty years of stability. While many sovereigns have struggled to provide a son, Edward's problem was that he had too many – seven in all. His first son, Edward (the 'Black Prince'), he created Duke of Cornwall, with two others, John and Lionel, becoming Dukes of Lancaster and Clarence respectively. When the heir to the throne died in 1376, he left his own ten-year-old son to succeed as Richard II. In due course, Richard gave dukedoms to the late king's other surviving sons, Edmund and Thomas. Thomas was made Duke of Gloucester, while Edmund became Duke of York. The titles were quite arbitrarily bestowed, having nothing to do with present-day county boundaries. And so, with Edmund, Duke of York, and John, Duke of Lancaster, the two rival clans were set for their mammoth trial of strength, with the Crown of England as the coveted first prize.

In fathering a healthy male progeny, upon whom he lavished extensive acreage and grand titles, Edward III had hoped to consolidate the family hold on the nation. In such circumstances, however, there is not safety in numbers. Where the inheritance of a kingdom is at stake, two is a crowd, probably a fact which came home to the patriarch in his declining years.

The rivalry, in its early stages, stopped short of armed conflict, both sides jockeying for position. The child king, Richard II, became a tool of the House of Lancaster, with John of Gaunt placing himself at the head of the Council of Regency. Already the Lancastrians were displaying a maniacal desire to rule – pre-empting a role traditionally reserved for Richard III. At this time, it suited all ambitious men to allow the young king to retain his role as a figurehead monarch, for these were difficult years. The ravages of the Black Death had created enormous social problems culminating in Wat Tyler's Peasants' Revolt in 1381. Rising to the occasion, Richard took Tyler by the horns and the revolt was savagely repressed. Gaining confidence from this success, Richard no longer wished to be 'guided' by his councillors. Not without reason did he consider himself fitted to rule, unhampered by his uncle, John of Gaunt's advice.

Richard's chief protagonist was not John of Gaunt himself, but the latter's son, Henry of Bolingbroke. Matters came to a head when Richard first banished Henry and, following John of Gaunt's death, then seized the Lancaster estates. In 1399 Henry returned to claim his inheritance. Richard, whose rule had become more and more dictatorial, found himself without supporters, and was deposed. Thus, Henry of Bolingbroke became Henry IV, and Lancastrian supremacy was established.

Under Lancastrian rule, the power of the nobles underwent a period of rapid growth. This was satisfactory, provided a strong monarch presided over all, which was the case during the reign of Henry V, whose conquests in France held the nation's attention. However, when the infant Henry VI came to the throne in 1422, the rivalries and mismanagement of those who ruled in his name led to the loss of all Henry V had gained. With the return from the French wars of the most warlike nobles and their followers, the pre-conditions for civil war were complete, and in 1452 Richard, Duke of York, returned from his lieutenancy of Ireland to throw down the gauntlet.

# Warfare in the Age of the Wars of the Roses

During the period of the Wars of the Roses, the raising of an army was a matter for private enterprise. This absolved the ruling monarch from the responsibility of maintaining a standing army which, as will become clear, was a luxury he could not afford. As the occasion arose armies would be raised by noblemen – for a price. When Englishmen or, at least, those of one's persuasion were not available, then mercenaries from Europe or, more commonly, Scotland would be employed. The system worked when a united kingdom was fighting a foreign war, but in times of civil conflict when treachery was prevalent, troops raised in the king's name might subsequently be used against him. Thus, the ruling dynasty would be keen to show favour to rebel nobles, in order to secure future support.

Armies comprised several component parts. At the top were the knights, clad in expensive armour and fighting either on horseback or on foot. At the other end were the archers – the fifteenth-century equivalent of artillery, without which an army could be at a serious disadvantage. Between the two was the infantry. Sometimes, the common soldier would go without payment, the agreement being that he would have the right to plunder. Usually, troops were deployed into three formations or 'battles': vanguard, centre and rearguard. All were important, and a weak formation could lose a battle. The Earl of Northumberland's inactivity as rearguard commander at Bosworth, for example, cost Richard III his crown.

A variety of weaponry existed, ranging from lances and swords to maces and axes, with the poorest combatants wielding anything that came to hand. The most effective long-range weapon was the longbow. In theory, all freemen between the ages of sixteen and sixty were under an obligation to engage in longbow practice. While the law was often ignored, the standard of bowmanship remained high, or at least good enough to prohibit general use of the crossbow and to defer development of firearms.

The extent to which artillery was used in the Wars of the Roses is unclear. Although cannon existed, they were not put to any great use on the field of battle, except in siege warfare. (This remained the case during the later English Civil War, at the outbreak of which the longbow actually reappeared as a weapon.) It is recorded that in Henry IV's siege of Berwick Castle in 1405, cannon, with stone projectiles, were used to considerable effect. Towards the end of the fifteenth century, iron cannon-balls came into use and builders of castles began to incorporate gunloops in their designs. Richard III made provision for artillery in alterations carried out at Warwick Castle, for example. On the whole, however, during the early fifteenth century, artillery was something to be utilized on overseas expeditions.

Edward IV appears to have recognized the potential of gunpowder. In 1469, at Losecoat Field (see p. 39), he put the rebels to flight with a show of cannon fire, while in 1471, on his return to England, he brought with him Flemish mercenaries armed with hand-guns – doubtless forerunners of the harquebus. By 1485, the possession of field artillery was essential, even if it was not overly used. Thus, although both Henry and Richard fought with cannon – and cannon-balls have been found at Bosworth Field – it could not be argued that artillery played a vital role in the end result.

# 3
# THE BATTLE OF EDGCOTE
## 26 July 1469

## *The Road to Edgcote*

Instability is one of the more obvious features of the Wars of the Roses. Armies had to be raised quickly in order to meet constant threats to the two principal power bases, York and Lancaster. There was by no means any guarantee that previous allies would lend their support in any new dispute. Loyalties remained mixed and changeable. As the struggle remained precariously balanced, the advantage would swing endlessly back and forth. The collapse of the Yorkist challenge at Ludlow in 1459 was followed by a Yorkist victory, with the capture of Henry VI, at Northampton, in July 1460. Five months later, the Yorkists were crushed at Wakefield, a battle that left the Duke of York's head adorning the York City gate. Despite a further defeat at the Second Battle of St Albans in February 1461, the late Duke of York's son, Edward, acceded as Edward IV on 4 March. Later in the month, he trounced the Lancastrians at Towton. The spring of 1464 saw him conducting a vigorous campaign against Lancastrian insurrection in the north of England, his success leading to a state of comparative peace until the summer of 1469.

Henry VI, confined to the Tower in 1465, had not been a strong king. True, in Margaret of Anjou (forced into exile in France) he had a strong-willed queen, but the administration was soundly lacking in skills of financial management, failings that became more pronounced with the mounting costs of almost continuous warfare. When such funds as Margaret was able to prise out of the French dried up, the Lancastrian cause floundered.

Edward IV, on the other hand, suffered from something of an excess of confidence. He began his reign by creating a new nobility on which he could depend for support. Inevitably, in his quest for a broader power base, he offended old partners, compounding the offence by his marriage to Elizabeth Woodville, whose husband had died fighting at the Second Battle of St Albans – on the Lancastrian side. The marriage took place in secret, and Edward must have known how it would be viewed by the Earl of Warwick, Richard Neville, who had been negotiating for a French marriage for the king. Perhaps Edward considered his position sufficiently secure to take the risk. Certainly, well aware of his predecessor's failings, he spent much time in improving the Crown's financial status, building up a sizeable interest in confiscated Lancastrian estates. In fact, he laid much of the groundwork for the creation of a stable monarchy and, in this respect, pre-empted Henry VII, to whom historians have perhaps unfairly ascribed much of the credit.

When it came, the split with Warwick was due, ostensibly, to differences of opinion in foreign policy. While Edward's preference was to pursue closer ties with the Duchy of Burgundy, Warwick wished to conclude an alliance with France. Matters came to a head when the king announced the engagement of his sister to the Duke of Burgundy. There followed a tripartite agreement between England, Burgundy and the Duchy of Brittany and hostilities with France appeared imminent. Warwick, meanwhile, had not been idle, having brokered a marriage himself between his elder daughter and Edward's brother (heir-presumptive to the throne), George, Duke of Clarence. The ceremony took place in Calais on 11 July 1469. Warwick, 'the Kingmaker', it appeared, was about to make another king.

# The Battle of Edgcote

As well as attempting to forge links abroad, it seems that the Earl of Warwick had also managed to oversee events at home. Lancastrians, aware of rifts developing in the Yorkists camp, were quick to incite riot where there had once been only discontent, and shrewd observers were of the opinion that Warwick himself was responsible. The most successful risings, based on perennial complaints about taxation, occurred in the north and were led, ostensibly, by the 'two Robins' – Robin of Redesdale and Robin of Holderness. The latter was defeated at York and subsequently executed, but his namesake proved more resilient, leaving Edward with no option but to mount a large-scale offensive.

During the summer of 1469, the king moved north, accumulating an army as he went. By the time he reached Nottingham, he had recruited fifteen thousand men but, on learning that Robin of Redesdale was in command of a well-disciplined army as opposed to a poorly-drilled rabble, he decided to await reinforcements – namely from the Earls of Devon and Pembroke, marching to join him from the west. Meanwhile, Warwick had returned from Calais and was at the head of a large army, marching swiftly north from Kent. Although Edward appreciated the consequences of being caught between Warwick and Redesdale, he was not to know that, upon reaching Banbury, Pembroke and Devonshire had fallen out. Devon reacted by withdrawing his six thousand men to the comparative safety of Deddington, while Pembroke took up a forward position to the south of Chipping Warden, in a valley known locally as Danes Moor.

Danes Moor is not really a moor at all. Although the name might conjure up impressions of a bleak, windswept landscape, bristling with heather and relieved only by occasional outcrops of jagged rocks, it is, in fact, a well-sheltered valley, surrounded by hills. Its location is one of the very reasons why Pembroke chose it for an overnight campsite. Taking into account the time of the year, he might have selected the higher ground towards Culworth which, although more exposed, has more to recommend it from a tactical point of view. Perhaps, unlike Edward, the earl was still working on the presumption that the rebel army was little more than a disorganized mob. If so, then it was an error of judgement for which he was to pay dearly.

Presumably, pickets were posted on the hills. If so, then their own carelessness cost them their lives, for the camp awoke on the morning of 26 July 1469 to find itself surrounded by Redesdale's men. The first reaction was one of panic, after which Pembroke was aware that decisive action would be necessary to avoid a rout. His position was further weakened by the fact that Devon had most of the archers with him at Deddington, and if he were to fight his way out (which appeared to be the only option open to him) the 'artillery' cover provided by concentrated ranks of longbow archers was an essential prerequisite. Since there were few archers, a break-out had to be attempted anyway.

At the head of his troops, Pembroke fought his way, inch by inch, to the summit of Edgcote Hill. As might be expected, casualties were high and by the time the Yorkists gained their objective, they must have been nearing exhaustion. However, they could not afford to relax. The temptation to retreat down the other side of the hill towards Wardington must have been great but somehow Pembroke managed to maintain discipline, his own conduct spreading confidence through the ranks. Once the high ground had been attained, however, the going was easier, and the rebels were pressed back along the ridge towards Thorpe Mandeville.

By this time it seemed that the unthinkable had happened and that the Yorkists were on the verge of converting a seemingly certain disaster into a famous victory. Keeping up the pressure and at the head of thinning ranks, Pembroke continued to push forward towards Culworth. Here, Redesdale's men were grouped in strength and the Yorkists began to falter, having to launch their assault against a very sharp incline. While containing the spearhead of Pembroke's attack, the rebels descended the hill on the

Sir William Herbert, Earl of Pembroke, and his wife, pay homage to Edward IV in this illustration from Lydgate's 'Troy Book' (Trustees of the British Museum)

Yorkists' flanks and Pembroke, who had miraculously survived serious injury, found himself becoming embroiled in personal combat.

As an apparently endless supply of rebels came pouring over the crest of the hill, the cry went up, 'A Warwick! A Warwick!', which Pembroke's men assumed meant that the Earl of Warwick's army was approaching Culworth. This proved too much for the battle-weary Yorkist survivors, who turned tail and retreated. Pursued by the rebels, they were disposed of in piecemeal fashion as they headed for Trafford Bridge and the River Cherwell. Pembroke fought on, hoping, perhaps, for an honourable death, but was eventually captured and afterwards beheaded. Devon, who by this time was approaching from Deddington, realized he was too late and beat a far less honourable retreat.

## The Aftermath

From Nottingham, the king had retreated south. Most sources agree that he was at Olney in Buckinghamshire when news of Edgcote reached him. In fact, he may have been further west, in the vicinity of Coventry. News of the

Pembroke's assault on this ridge overlooking Culworth was to end in defeat

defeat filtered through to his army, which promptly deserted, leaving him with no choice but to appeal, cap in hand, to his old mentor, Warwick. The kingmaker's response was to send his brother, the Archbishop of York, to take his monarch into custody. Under armed guard, Edward was taken first to Coventry and then on to Warwick Castle, where the earl was at pains to reassert his authority in what he saw as a master and pupil relationship.

Meanwhile, the hunt for leading Yorkists continued. Earl Rivers and Sir John Woodville were apprehended in the Forest of Dean and beheaded at Gosford Green, near Coventry. The Earl of Devon was finally executed at Bridgwater. Warwick's power now seemed at its zenith. He held two kings of England captive – Henry in the Tower and Edward at Middleham Castle, to which he was moved on 25 August – and as their captor, Warwick was in a strong position to decide who should retain the title.

Henry was a plausible choice, but his administration had proved a failure. Edward had been more successful but, as recent events had shown, his liking for independence could pose a threat. There were some who thought Warwick himself had designs on the throne – suspicions which, in the end, would lead to his downfall – and to install Clarence, the heir-presumptive, as a puppet-king would be too obvious a move. As it happened, factors outside Warwick's control eventually forced his hand.

Edward was persuaded to condemn disturbances in London, giving the impression that he was still in command. A more serious insurrection on the Scottish borders, headed by Humphrey Neville, proved more difficult to handle. Warwick struggled to raise an army on his own account and Edward had to be freed. Still under supervision, he was put on display in York, troops were raised in his name and the Scottish revolt was put down. Humphrey Neville was beheaded in York on 29 September. Apparently satisfied with Edward's protestations of loyalty, Warwick allowed him to return to the capital, alone.

There now developed a stand-off situation, Warwick choosing to remain absent from London in view of Edward's popularity. For his part, Edward realized that popularity, in itself, did not guarantee his position. For the time being, he remained content to build up his strength by filling influential posts with loyal appointees. Ideally, he wanted Warwick in London and in December, accompanied by a strong retinue, the kingmaker finally acquiesced, realizing that he could not keep his distance indefinitely. At a specially convened Council meeting, Warwick agreed to recognize Edward as his sovereign. In return, Edward granted a pardon to all who had risen against him. Outwardly, therefore, it seemed the hatchet had been buried. However, both parties to the agreement knew that this could never be. Where there had once been trust, there was now suspicion. Where there had once been friendship, there was now resentment. For Warwick, this was coupled with the knowledge that in less than five months his position had been transformed from conqueror to servant of the vanquished. He had won the war, but lost the peace. And Edward knew that as long as Warwick lived, he would never be master in his own kingdom.

# *The Walk*

**Distance:**   7 miles (11 km)

The starting point is the village of Wardington (Landranger 151 4946), to the north-east of Banbury. Off-road parking is available by the Hare and Hounds at the north end of the village at the corner of the Edgcote road (point A).

Set off towards Edgcote, ignoring any inviting stiles to the right. (The first stile in line introduces a path alongside a stream – a tributary of the River Cherwell – leading to the rear of the village, parallel with the A361). A little way ahead a wooden post indicates a public footpath to the right, although the post is without its 'public footpath' arrow (point B). Climb the gate and enter the field, keeping close to the hedgerow. (Some of the gates to be

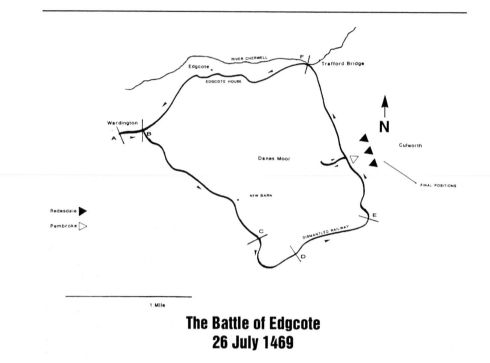

1 Mile

## The Battle of Edgcote
## 26 July 1469

negotiated throughout this walk are old, rusted and will not open, and care is needed in climbing them.) This is the beginning of a more or less straight 3 mile stretch. For the first field or two, the going is easy, but it gets tougher as one progresses to ploughed fields.

A comfortable climb of just over a mile brings the crest of the hill into view. I like to pause at this spot to look back and survey Wardington with the aid of binoculars. Now look to the left, to the highest point on the hill, which falls down steeply to Danes Moor. Walk on, past the farm buildings on the left to the point where the path and a farm track cross (point C). The farm track runs down to the road on the right. The path should be straight ahead, but barbed wire and a ploughed field make it impractical, so follow the farm track down to the road.

The farm track meets the road at a bridge (Pathfinder 1022 513451) which crosses the old Banbury to Culworth Junction railway line. Careful negotiation of a couple of gates on the left will lead to the railway embankment. Walking along the embankment is quite easy because a path – the public right of way for future generations of ramblers – is being beaten through the undergrowth. Further along, there is a gap in the hedge, which would have been the point of entry if the original footpath over the field had not been ploughed up.

Keep on to the metal footbridge (point D), which has to be crossed as here the path is actually barred by fencing and barbed wire. Turning to the left, proceed along the embankment, rather impeded by undergrowth, and carefully scramble down the embankment and on to the bed of the railway track, where the going becomes considerably easier.

Railway walks are a discipline in their own right, and there is a lot to be said for the opportunities presented by the ready-made paths of disused lines. The present line was part of the Great Central Railway, connecting Banbury, Chalcombe and Eydon to the main north–south Great Central arterial line. The branch line opened in 1900 with a double track and great expectations for both goods and passenger traffic. It survived until 1956.

The track runs beneath a second bridge – this time an attractive ivy-clad brick structure. A little further on is a third (brick) bridge and this is where one should leave the line (point E). Although the track bed has been levelling out as you have progressed, the bridge still looms above. This is because the approach to it on either side is by a raised embankment. Scramble up the embankment to the left. In the far corner, between bridge and field, squeeze carefully through into the field, aiming for the straight path along the hedgerow to the right. (The raised path leading to the bridge behind presents a most curious sight, being both gated and overgrown with trees and shrubbery. Unlike today's road makers, the Grand Central engineers ensured that there was no shortage of crossing points over their thoroughfares.)

The escarpment to the right is most prominent. Ahead, on rising ground to the left, are some ruined farm buildings. When one reaches the hedgerow which backs them, take a detour towards them – the nearside of the hedge is also a footpath. When one reaches the ruins (Pathfinder 1022 523466), on the crest of a hill, one can look down on Danes Moor – a snug spot for a camp. The climb will have been deceptively steep, so consider the strain on the Yorkists, forced to take an uphill fight to the rebels.

Retracing one's steps (appreciating the advantage conferred on an army which could build up momentum when charging downhill), turn left at the bottom. Keep going, past the farm buildings and scrapyard on the right to arrive at a small grazing field (which may contain sheep). The Culworth road is ahead. Scramble over one of the fences on the right and emerge on to a road, turning left, to approach Trafford Bridge (point F) where many of the fleeing Yorkists were cut down by their pursuers as they tried to cross the river. At the bridge, take the single-track road signposted to Edgcote – a straight run of about 1½ miles. To the right, Edgcote House (Pathfinder 1022 506479) comes into view.

The house was built on the site of an older house, over a five-year period from 1747 to 1752 and at a cost of just over £20,000. Charles I is said to have spent the nights both before and after the Battle of Edgehill (see p. 82)

Edgcote House

in the original house. There was also a village, demolished later in the eighteenth century to make way for a landscaped park. The area retains a curious tranquility.

Turning past the Edgcote estate one is on the home stretch to Wardington. Continue to the Hare and Hounds for some well-earned refreshments.

## *Further Explorations*

Edgcote is but a short distance from Cropredy (Landranger 151 4646). The Civil War engagement on 29 June 1644 at Cropredy Bridge is covered later in this volume (see pp. 111–20) and a visit to the area might take in both battlefields. Many of the potential further explorations are common to both locations.

It is possible to walk by the Edgcote estate and into Chipping Norton – a pleasant walk in itself. However, there are other houses in the area, open to visitors, which may also be of interest.

Sulgrave (Landranger 152 5545), to the east of Edgcote, has connections with a different war in a different country. Sulgrave Manor was built in the mid-sixteenth century by a wealthy wool merchant and sometime mayor of Northampton, Lawrence Washington. His great-great-grandson, John Washington, emigrated to America in the mid-seventeenth century and settled in Virginia where, in 1732, the first American president was born. Sulgrave Manor is therefore a place of pilgrimage for many American tourists, who can combine a trip to Sulgrave with visits to USAAF wartime airfields in Northamptonshire. Opened to the public in 1921, the house, which is quite small, has been lovingly restored. Sulgrave Manor is open throughout the year. For more details, telephone (0295) 760205. St James's church in the village also contains much in the way of Washington memorabilia.

Weedon Lois (Landranger 152 5946), which the inhabitants like to call Lois Weedon, has a churchyard in which the poet and eccentric Edith Sitwell is buried. The church itself bears a plaque telling the brief story of one William Losse, a priest at the time of the Civil War. Roundhead troops, furious at Losse's refusal to submit to them, riddled him with pistol fire and then butchered him with their swords, at the top of the church tower.

Grafton Regis (Landranger 152 7546), although only a hamlet, has an importance far outweighing its size, for it was the home of the Woodvilles. Prominent players in the Wars of the Roses, the family provided a queen, Elizabeth, for Edward IV. Grafton Regis was also the scene of a Civil War battle. Held for the Royalists by Sir John Digby, it was a thorn in the Parliamentarian flesh, a base from which operations to harass Roundhead lines of communications between Northampton and the West Country were launched. On 21 December 1643, one thousand Roundhead troops under the command of Sgt.-Major-General Philip Skippon, invested the manor-house and, after three days of fierce fighting, succeeded in pounding the village into submission – finishing off the job by firing the manor. Three hundred years later, on 21 December 1943, six Irish agricultural labourers occupied a caravan on the site of the battle. During the night, they were awakened by the sounds of battle – charging horses, gunfire and the cries of the combatants – which continued for an hour or more. Too terrified to move, they were found by their supervisor, still huddled together in their caravan, the following morning. Their story was given short shrift by many, who preferred to believe that the men had invented an excuse for having overslept, following a night at the White Hart. However, it does seem to be a strange story for anyone to have concocted, particularly when one considers that the Irishmen are unlikely to have heard of what was a little-known skirmish.

# Further Information

Despite the coming of the railway (now defunct) and the motorway (M40), Danes Moor has retained its rural character. However, road communications are good, Wardington lying to the north-east of Banbury on the A361, which itself feeds into the M40 at junction 11.

For British Rail services to the area call Banbury (0295) 260256. National Express coach services information is available on 021 622 4373. For local bus services call Banbury (0295) 262368.

Landranger 151 and Pathfinder 1022 cover the entire battlefield area, while Landranger 152 will also be needed for further exploration. Edgcote is a battle on which comparatively little has been written. Philip Warner's *British Battlefields: The Midlands* (Osprey 1973) contains a readable account.

# 4
# THE BATTLE OF EMPINGHAM
## 12 March 1470

## *The Road to Empingham*

The mutual distrust between Edward IV and the Earl of Warwick, in the aftermath of Edgcote, simmered throughout the early months of 1470. From time to time, there occurred sundry conflicts between rival families – little more than outbreaks of domestic violence of no real import to Lancastrian or Yorkist ambitions, whatever the persuasion of the combatants. Of much greater significance, however, were disturbances in Lincolnshire engineered, it seems, by Warwick and Clarence.

The disturbances were fronted by Richard, Lord Welles, and his son, Sir Robert, assisted by Lord Welles' brother-in-law, Sir Thomas Dimmock. Based at Alford, the Welles, who were related to Warwick, could trace their ancestry back to the Norman Conquest. A member of the king's household, Sir Thomas Burgh, of Gainsborough, was a comparative newcomer to the county nobility and, resenting Burgh's elevation to high office, Lord Welles had demolished his house. At length, Edward summoned Welles and Dimmock to the capital but, fearing the king's wrath, both claimed sanctuary in Westminster Abbey.

The disturbances provided Edward with opportunities of his own. His personal intervention would help to restore some of the authority he had lost at Edgcote. Accordingly, on 6 March, having given instructions for troops to assemble at Grantham, he set out for Lincolnshire. He had got as far as Waltham Cross when word reached him that Sir Robert Welles was raising an army at Ranby, between Alford and Lincoln, with a view to offering resistance. Even at this stage, Edward seems to have trusted Warwick and Clarence, because he provided them with written authority to raise troops on his behalf.

At Huntingdon, Edward was joined by Dimmock and Welles the elder, whom he had sent for from London, and who had left the sanctuary of

Westminster Abbey on the promise of safe conduct. Under interrogation, they admitted their part in a conspiracy to overthrow the king, and Welles was forced to write to his son, ordering him to give himself up if he wished to save both his father's and Dimmock's lives. Upon reaching Fotheringhay, Edward learned that such an army as Sir Robert had managed to muster was marching south of Grantham. In fact, the rebels veered off towards Leicester where Warwick and Clarence had arranged to meet them, only to turn back eastwards when Sir Robert received his father's letter. However, rather than submit to the king, Sir Robert decided to give battle, although he must have known that Edward's first move would be to carry out his threat. When the king reached Stamford on 12 March, that is exactly what he did. Some say that Lord Welles and Dimmock were beheaded in the market-place at Stamford, others that the executions were performed in front of the rebel army on the battlefield. Much has been made of this action, considering that Edward had originally guaranteed the victims' safety.

The rebels' march on Stamford dashed Edward's hopes of his own rendezvous at Grantham. Despite the promises of support from Warwick and Clarence, who were supposed to be marching to his aid with whatever troops they were able to raise, Edward must, by now, have entertained serious doubts as to the extent to which he could depend upon the support of his erstwhile friends.

## The Battle of Empingham

Edward's scouts lost no time in advising him of the approach of the rebel army towards Stamford, leaving the king to ponder Sir Robert's next move. In fact, there was to be no attack on Stamford itself, the rebels stopping 5 miles short of the town and it was here, along the ridge of high ground slightly to the north of the present-day Tickencote Warren, that Sir Robert deployed his men. It is unlikely that the army gathered much local support, as Stamford was strongly Yorkist – sentiments no doubt encouraged by the presence of Edward's troops. All available local manpower had been mobilized before the rebels' arrival, with the leading families in the area, such as the Mackworths of Empingham, lending their weight to the Yorkist cause.

The total strength of the rebel force is difficult to estimate. Clearly, it was not as large as Sir Robert would have hoped. With little or no local support available and, most significantly, without Warwick and Clarence whom, it was apparent, would not be appearing for them, the rebels' chances of success were slim. The highest contemporary estimate of rebel numbers is

This portrait of Edward IV, by an unknown artist, belies his reputation as a fighting man, ready at all times (as at Empingham) to take the battle to the enemy (Royal Collection)

put at around thirty thousand, but the total is more likely to have been less than half that number, especially when one allows for the probability of the disaffected slipping away as the prospect of a battle loomed ahead.

Edward's army may not have been substantially larger, but it would have been better fed and armed. The king must have been aware of the relatively poor condition of the opposition, for he chose to take the battle to them, marching out of Stamford on the morning of 12 March 1470, to attack the strong defensive position Sir Robert had selected.

What happened next is open to conjecture. Edward had a number of cannon, which were dragged laboriously up the Casterton Road towards Tickencote. The Yorkists' progress must have been slow and the rebel Lancastrians, drawn up squarely across the present-day A1, presumably watched them coming on. As soon as the rebels were within range, the artillery was made ready and several salvos were fired into the massed Lancastrian ranks. Apparently, the damage wrought by the guns was sufficient to strike terror into the hearts of the rebels, who had doubtless hoped to harass the Yorkists as they drew nearer. In fact, the cannon fire was probably inaccurate and may not have caused a great deal in the way of death and destruction. But it did give the impression of superior strength, which no doubt did much to further discourage the poorly-disciplined rebels.

In the confusion that the cannon fire created, the Yorkists took the opportunity to launch an all-out assault on the enemy positions. That there was some resistance is proved by rebels' cries of 'A Clarence! A Warwick!', designed to rally the troops, but as the Yorkists' cavalry reached the ridge, all opposition collapsed. It is said that the panic-stricken rebels, in their haste to escape, cast away their jackets, thus giving the confrontation its alternative title, 'The Battle of Losecoat Field'. In the hope of not being identified by their pursuers, it is possible that some rebels – for example, Sir Robert's own retainers, who would have worn his livery – did throw away their coats. Others may have worn emblems identifying them with the rebel army, and these may have been torn hurriedly from jackets and headgear.

Sir Robert was subsequently captured, but the slaughter of the fleeing rebels must have been great, many being cut down in the wood, which has retained the name 'Bloody Oaks' and which is still allegedly haunted by the cries of the dying.

## *The Aftermath*

The Battle of Empingham may have been short, but the result was of immense significance for both sides. On the following day, Edward wrote to Warwick and Clarence, ordering them to join him without delay at Grantham, accompanied by a small escort only. At Coventry, they told the king's messenger that they would certainly make all haste to Grantham – and promptly took off in the opposite direction, hoping to take advantage of continuing disturbances in the north. Perhaps this had always been a reserve option in the event of the Lincolnshire venture going wrong. On 17 March, when Edward had reached Newark, he received further missives from the prodigals (who had reached Chesterfield, via Burton upon Trent and Derby) promising to meet him at Retford. At this point, Edward decided on a more direct approach, advising them that if they failed to surrender themselves, he would take them by force of arms. At the head of his own army once more, he felt sufficiently confident to throw down the gauntlet. Despite his promise of fair treatment, Warwick and Clarence (mindful, no doubt, of the guarantees extended to Lord Welles and Dimmock) moved on to Manchester, to seek the support of Lord Stanley, who refused to commit himself.

On 19 March, Sir Robert Welles was executed, having given a full confession, which implicated Warwick and Clarence in the Lincolnshire rising. Edward claimed that Sir Robert was not under duress, and had confessed of his own free will. This may be true and, whereas Warwick was undoubtedly prepared to encourage unrest for his own ends, it is probably also true that Edward was at pains to exaggerate further the extent of his complicity. Following Sir Robert's confession, conspirators at a provincial level, such as Robin of Redesdale, who had thrown themselves on the king's mercy, also became keen to apportion as much of the blame as possible to Warwick who, after all, had abandoned them to their fate.

His patience at an end – and at last feeling strong enough to do so – Edward declared Warwick and Clarence to be traitors and posted rewards for their capture. He also had the presence of mind to cut off the traditional escape routes by warning the garrisons in Dublin and Calais of the situation. Indeed, it was for Calais that the outcasts were bound. From Manchester, they marched to Warwick Castle, where they gathered the earl's portable goods and chattels. Accompanied by a substantial retinue of several thousand men, they turned west to Exeter and, ultimately, to Dartmouth, where, on 10 April, they set sail for Calais. Four days later, Edward arrived from York, only to find that his quarry had once more evaded him.

Warwick's welcome at Calais was rather less enthusiastic than he had hoped. In fact, he and Clarence were refused entry, the dialogue between Warwick and the garrison deteriorating into an exchange of cannon fire. Their fortunes, it seemed, had finally turned. In the end, Warwick was forced to sail further along the French coast, eventually arriving in Honfleur on 1 May. He appealed to Louis for sanctuary and, to his immense relief, Louis obliged.

In England, a firm line was taken with many of the rebels who had not effected their escape, the Earl of Worcester doing much to earn his nickname of 'the butcher'. Those who had proved more loyal subjects, were rewarded. Having at last shaken off the chains of his mentor, Edward seemed, for the moment, to have re-established his authority as King of England. And a brief moment it would prove to be for, within the year, the tables once more would be turned.

# The Walk

**Distance:**   8 miles (13 km)

This is a walk for the connoisseur, demonstrating the importance of on-site experience for anyone who wishes to understand how battles were won and lost.

Begin in Empingham (Landranger 141 9508). The village is approached by the A606 Stamford to Oakham road. There is only one main street running through the village and the starting point is the post office

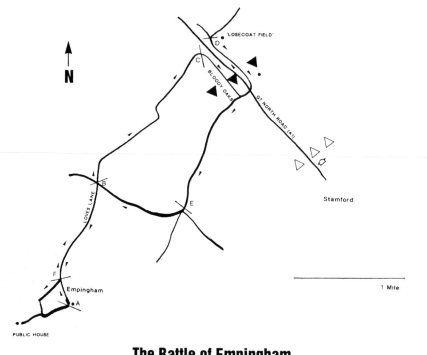

## The Battle of Empingham
## 12 March 1470

(Pathfinder 896 953088) (point A). If arriving by bus, one alights nearby. If driving, park a little further west by the medical centre in Willoughby Drive.

The post office is at the corner of Loves Lane. Walk up Loves Lane, a single-track road, which climbs steadily out of the village. After about a mile (moving on to Pathfinder 876) one arrives at an unmarked crossroads (point B). To the left is Exton, to the right, Tickencote. Go straight ahead, through the gate, to follow the signposted bridle-path. The path runs past Empingham Old Wood and Old Wood Lodge Farm (Pathfinder 896 958105), guarded by dogs, which are usually kennelled.

When the fields open up the track bears sharply to the left before becoming straight once more. Ahead is the A1. While it is now seen largely as a relief road for the motorway, there has been some talk of expanding this road from a dual to a three-lane carriageway, which could lead to the ruination of yet another important battlefield.

To the right, bordering the A1, is more woodland. This is Bloody Oaks (Pathfinder 896 975115) (point C) which, according to local tradition, acquired its name by the slaughter of the rebel army on the site. The bridle-way comes to an abrupt end at the A1. Climb the fence ahead and follow

A view over Losecoat Field, looking towards Stamford. Bloody Oaks is on the right. Welles's rebels were probably deployed along the ridge beyond the thin line of trees

the verge to the right for about 500 yd. Depending upon the season of one's visit, this may involve picking one's way through some shrubbery. Look over to Bloody Oaks, which presents a curiously lifeless and decaying picture. At the end of the wood is the main Empingham road. To the left is the underpass running beneath the A1. Cross over (with care) and use the underpass, walking on the path provided. At the other side, turn to the left (again with care, for this is a slip-road servicing the A1, though not usually too busy) and follow the road.

Approaching the road to Pickworth, branching off to the right, one is walking parallel with the field that is generally accepted to be the site of the battle (point D). To the left, and slightly to the rear, at the other side of the A1 is Bloody Oaks. Looking back down the road, one can see very little, and it seems a curious spot for a battle to be fought. In fact, the lie of the land suggests that such fighting as did take place occurred a little closer to Stamford. Turning back and looking up to the left, one can see that the land rises to a crest at a point where the Bloody Oaks walk was drawing to a close. It is more likely that the rebels were drawn up on this ridge and that they advanced towards Stamford to meet Edward, marching up Ermine Street. Clearly this walk illustrates the difficulties encountered when attempting to appreciate troop movements in a landscape subject to continuous change.

Now walk back to the underpass, following the road straight ahead, in the direction of Empingham. Just over a mile ahead is a crossroads (point E). Take the right-hand fork and continue to a left turn, which takes one on to Loves Lane. Instead of following the road down into Empingham, take the signposted bridle-path off to the right, where the road curves (point F). It is a pleasure to use this path. The gate opens easily, while ploughing has not been extended to the hedgerow. Instead, there is a wide grass path which makes for easy walking. Having made adequate provision for ramblers and horses, the farmer reaps his reward as everyone keeps to the path and his crops are undisturbed. (Passing the farm buildings to the left, look out for the dovecote standing alone in a field.)

The path leads to the Exton road. Turn left and walk to the crossroads and turn right. This will lead to the Hare and Hounds, where refreshments are available if required. The starting point can be regained by turning left from the inn and following the road.

## Further Explorations

To fully appreciate the layout of the battle, further exploration is necessary. Take the Pickworth road, which runs near the site of Woodhead Castle (Pathfinder 876 997116). From this point, one has a clear view of both Yorkist and Lancastrian positions. The castle had fallen into disrepair as early as 1543. Very little of Pickworth (Pathfinder 876 993138) remains, destroyed, according to local tradition, by the combatants.

Stamford itself is of interest because it was sacked in April 1461 by Margaret's Lancastrian army en route to St Albans. The damage inflicted then is often given as the cause of Stamford's subsequent decline – although the fluctuating fortunes of the wool trade may be a more accurate reason. In any event, this harsh treatment confirmed the town in its Yorkist sympathies, and it rallied to Edward IV's cause nine years later, earning the right to use the royal coat of arms on the borough shield.

One mile to the south-east of Stamford stands Burghley House (tel: 0780 52451) (Landranger 141 0406). Built between 1565 and 1587 by William Cecil, adviser to Queen Elizabeth I, it has remained the home of the Cecil family for over four hundred years. In July 1643, Burghley found itself weathering a short siege when a group of Royalists, retreating from an engagement at Peterborough, took refuge there. Their tactful surrender saved the house from destruction by Cromwell's artillery.

One of the newer long-distance footpaths, the Viking Way, also skirts the area. It runs from Barton-upon-Humber, in South Humberside, to

Oakham, in Rutland, a total of 130 miles. The route is marked on Pathfinder 876 (931123) and acquires its name from the Danish invasions of the area in the ninth century. Another path, the Hereward Way (Pathfinder 896 958082), actually runs through Empingham and celebrates East Anglia's folk-hero, Hereward the Wake. Neither route takes in Losecoat field.

# *Further Information*

Empingham can be found on the A606 Stamford to Oakham road, the most straightforward approach being by way of the A1.

The village is also accessible via British Rail, Stamford. Call Peterborough (0733) 68181 for details. For information on National Express coach services call 021 622 4373. Additional bus information is available from Leicester City Council Busline (tel: Leicester (0533) 511411) and Blands of Cottesmore (tel: Oakham (0572) 812220).

Ordnance Survey maps for the area are Landrangers 141 and 130 and Pathfinders 896 and 876. Opportunities for further reading are very limited, specific accounts of the fighting being buried in more general accounts of the rebellion. *The English Historical Review* of October 1988 and the *Camden Miscellany* of 1847 both contain excellent background information.

# 5
# THE BATTLE OF TEWKESBURY
## 4 May 1471

## *The Road to Tewkesbury*

Between May 1470 and 1471, events involving the Houses of York and Lancaster moved on apace. Warwick's arrival home from France in September 1470 drove Edward out of England. In March 1471, however, Edward returned and, on 14 April, at Barnet, regained his crown in Warwick's final battle. During his enforced exile, Warwick had made his peace with Margaret of Anjou, herself exiled in France, although she failed to respond to Warwick's repeated entreaties for her to join him to consolidate their position. She may have been awaiting favourable winds or purposely delaying until the outcome of the inevitable battle between Edward and Warwick was known, with a view to taking on the mauled victor and placing her own son, Prince Edward, on the throne. For whatever reason, she arrived too late to be of any help to Warwick, landing at Weymouth on the day of the contest at Barnet. The Countess of Warwick, aboard another ship, arrived at Southampton and, on learning of the disaster at Barnet, immediately took sanctuary at Beaulieu Abbey in the New Forest. Margaret made her way to Cerne Abbey, where she too was told of Warwick's defeat. At first, it appears that she thought it best to return to the protection of Louis. However, her supporters, including the Duke of Somerset and the Earl of Devon, seem to have had little difficulty in persuading her to stay and fight.

It was proposed to augment Margaret's army with another raised in the West Country and for these two groups to link up with more sympathizers from the north, so creating a force of sufficient strength to march on London – manoeuvres which would have provided Edward with valuable breathing space. As she moved through Wells and Bath, therefore, she tried to throw Edward off guard by spreading rumours that she was to launch an imminent assault on the capital. As he had successfully done before, so Edward resolved to take the battle to the enemy, however, and, on 24 April, he rode out of Windsor at the head of a revitalized army of Barnet veterans and enthusiastic new recruits. On 29 April, he was at Cirencester, advancing quickly to Malmesbury. By this time, Margaret had reached Bristol and, learning that Edward was so close, threw him another red herring by announcing that she intended to give battle at Sodbury Hill, a point between Bristol and Malmesbury. Consequently, Edward set out for Sodbury and spent the best part of 2 May waiting for Margaret. She, meanwhile, was advancing on Gloucester, with a view to crossing the Severn and linking up with Jasper Tudor, uncle of the future Henry VII, in Wales.

A forced march led Margaret to the gates of Gloucester on the morning of 3 May where, much to her consternation, she was refused entry. In order to cross the Severn, the only alternative was to travel a further 10 miles to Tewkesbury. During the course of this final exhaustive march, the cavalry began to draw away from the infantry while the artillery fell dangerously behind. On reaching Tewkesbury in the late afternoon of 3 May, Margaret realized that her army could go no further. With Edward now so close, there was little chance of effecting a swift crossing, and Margaret's only realistic option was to stand and fight.

There is some discord among historians as to the defensive site chosen by the Lancastrians. The most likely position is to the south of Tewkesbury at Gupshill. Gupshill occupies a low ridge which appears to have been the strongest position available to a tired army with its back to the wall. There was little that could be done to improve the natural advantages of the chosen ground. With battle almost certain to commence on the following day, rest for the weary troops was of paramount importance, the only major activity necessary being the planning of the order of battle. The army would be drawn up along the ridge, the Duke of Somerset commanding the right wing, with the Earl of Devon on the left and the young Prince Edward and Lord Wenlock in the centre.

The Yorkist army cannot have been less weary, for its march via Cheltenham, in a line parallel to that taken by the Lancastrians, was attended by its own share of hardship, particularly in terms of shortage of water and provisions. At about 4.00 p.m. on 3 May, Edward, determined to stop the proposed Lancastrian link-up with Jasper Tudor, arrived at the village of Tredlington, only 3 miles from Tewkesbury, where he too was thankful to be able to rest.

# *The Battle of Tewkesbury*

On the morning of 4 May, Edward mustered his six thousand men and opened hostilities, as was his wont. Richard, Duke of Gloucester, commanded his vanguard, Lord Hastings, the rearguard and Edward himself, accompanied by Clarence, the centre. Two hundred spearmen were positioned to the left on a wooded hill. The Lancastrians were subjected to an artillery and arrow barrage, the brunt of which appears to have been borne by Somerset's right wing. Perhaps as part of a set-piece, or maybe simply to relieve the pressure, Somerset advanced downhill to meet Gloucester. As luck would have it, his path took him more to his left, towards the Yorkist centre. Despite the suddenness of the onslaught, the Yorkist centre held. Somerset, however, remained unsupported and, when Gloucester attacked his right flank, his position became untenable. When the hidden Yorkist spearmen were called to action, the Lancastrians fled. As in all such instances, well-led disciplined troops fighting a rearguard action might well have retreated to a position of comparative safety, whereas to throw down one's arms and run, was tantamount to suicide. And so, many of those who sought only to save their lives were cut down in the lanes and in the ditches. It is said that Somerset himself regained his hilltop position and, in retribution for Wenlock's failure to support him, cleft his skull in two with a battleaxe.

Seizing his opportunity, Edward now took the offensive, in the face of which, Lancastrian resistance first faltered and then collapsed, the remains of the once ambitious army joining Somerset's division in wholesale retreat, to be cut down or drowned in their efforts to cross the Swillgate. The events

A contemporary representation of the Battle of Tewkesbury (University Library, Ghent)

that occurred in the field still called 'Bloody Meadow' may well be imagined. Somerset himself contrived to organize a last stand, but it proved ineffectual against the tide of the Yorkist advance, and soon even he chose escape in preference to a glorious death.

Escape for many of the Lancastrians, including Somerset, lay in claiming sanctuary in Tewkesbury Abbey and various other churches in the locality. Before the Battle of Empingham, Edward had called Lord Welles and Sir Thomas Dimmock out of sanctuary only to have them executed. On this occasion, his contempt for the concept of sanctuary was further demonstrated by the Yorkist invasion of Tewkesbury Abbey in search of those Lancastrians who had sought refuge within its walls. Somerset and the Earl of Devon were among those who were unceremoniously dragged out and shortly afterwards beheaded, the executions probably taking place at the cross in the town centre.

The fate of Margaret's son, Prince Edward, is in some doubt. In all probability he was killed in the fighting. An alternative, but unsubstantiated version of events has him brought before the king, in whose presence he is butchered by Gloucester and Clarence. Tradition allots two possible localities for this alleged atrocity – a shop in the High Street, near Tolsey Lane, or a house by the old cross, looking out to the market place. Margaret had expressed a preference for his non-involvement in the battle. Had she insisted, then his survival would have confirmed his role as a figurehead and future rallying point for Lancastrian sympathies.

The number of Lancastrian dead was probably in the region of fifteen hundred, with Yorkist losses of perhaps less than half this figure. Tewkesbury itself was pillaged, while surrounding churches which had given sanctuary to the fleeing Lancastrians were defiled. At Didbrook, near Winchcombe, for example, fugitives were pursued and butchered on site – an act which necessitated the rededication of the church.

# The Aftermath

On 7 May, the victorious Edward departed from Tewkesbury. With unrest simmering in the north and rapidly coming to the boil in Kent, he could not afford the luxury of reclining in victory. While en route to Worcester, he was encouraged to hear of the capture of Margaret, who had taken sanctuary at – most probably – Little Malvern Priory. She joined Edward at Coventry on 11 May and remained the king's captive until 1476, when she was permitted to return to France, where she lived in poverty until her death in 1492.

At Coventry, Edward learned that the disturbances in the north country had settled themselves, which left him free to concentrate on the rising in Kent, the contrivance of Thomas, bastard of Fauconberg, who had landed at Sandwich and was forcing the locals to join his motley, though substantial, band of ruffians in a march on the capital. In Edward's absence, the citizens did remarkably well – albeit in the interests of self-preservation rather than out of loyalty to their king – and Thomas's efforts to sack the city met with stiff opposition. Eventually, he was compelled to withdraw and, losing heart at the prospect of a pitched battle with the rapidly approaching king, he fled. Unable to make good his escape, he was executed before the year was out.

All Edward's enemies were now either dead or in custody. Had Warwick and Margaret combined forces, then he might well have been overthrown, although this should not be seen as lessening his achievement in disposing of each individually, and afterwards having the resolve to continue to subdue remaining pockets of resistance. The most far-reaching of Edward's post-war actions, however, took place upon his triumphal return to London on 21 May. Queen Margaret was paraded through the streets in a carriage – a fate which defeated warrior queens had usually avoided by the expedient of taking poison. At some time during the evening, the hapless ex-king Henry was found dead in the Tower. Despite Yorkist claims of a natural death, it is certain that he was murdered on Edward's orders. The following day, his body was displayed for the benefit of the public at large. It is reported that the corpse bled – a sure sign, according to those with an interest in such ghoulish matters, that Henry had met with a violent end. He was buried at Chertsey. Spending on the funeral arrangements was lavish.

The Wars of the Roses at last seemed to have drawn to a close, with the House of York victorious. For the next twelve years, Edward IV reigned supreme. Able to turn his attentions once more to the problems of peacetime government, he continued to try to accumulate wealth for the Crown and to create conditions in which trade and industry were able to grow and flourish. There remained only one potential problem – and at this point in time a very minor one. Following his unsuccessful attempt to link up with Margaret's army before Tewkesbury, Jasper Tudor and his nephew, Henry, Earl of Richmond, had taken refuge in Chepstow Castle. From there, they had retreated into Pembrokeshire. However, when it became clear that Edward intended to flush them out wherever they might try to secrete themselves, they escaped to Brittany, where they were to remain, in straitened circumstances, for the next fourteen years. Although Edward was at pains to keep a wary eye on them, he was not unduly worried. After all, what threat to Yorkist supremacy could ever be posed by an impoverished, exiled Tudor?

# *The Walk*

**Distance:**   4 miles (6½ km)

Start at the Tourist Office in Barton Street (point A) (Pathfinder 1042 895326), where information on the battle can be obtained. The building also houses the museum, containing a diorama of the battle.

Emerging from the Tourist Office, turn to the left to walk up Barton Street and, bearing left, on into Church Street and Tewkesbury Abbey (point B). The abbey contains the remains of Edward, Prince of Wales, the most celebrated casualty of the Battle of Tewkesbury, and also of George, Duke of Clarence. To derive most benefit from the walk, a visit to the abbey should not be missed. As events are sometimes staged there which make this awkward, if not impossible, it is wise to call before setting out (tel: (0684) 850959).

From the abbey, turn to the left, continuing down Church Street, bearing left on to Gloucester Road. Shortly after crossing the River Swilgate, Lower Lode Lane branches off to the right and parkland (known as The Vineyards) runs away to the left. One scenario for the battle has the Lancastrians ranged out across the road at this point – Prince Edward in the centre, flanked by Devonshire on the left and Somerset on the right. Continue down Gloucester Road (the A38), which has a good footpath,

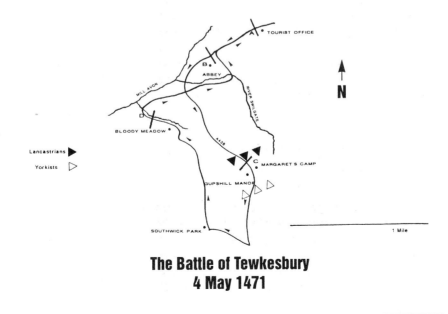

## The Battle of Tewkesbury
## 4 May 1471

and, to the south of Lincoln Green Lane, the likely Yorkist position is encountered (Edward IV in the centre, with Gloucester on his left and Hastings on his right).

Continue as far as Gupshill Manor public house (Pathfinder 1042 894314). If the alternative site for the conflict is accepted, it is feasible that this house, built in 1438, stood in the centre of the battleground, sandwiched between Lancastrians, slightly to the north, and Yorkists, to the south. Queen Margaret is reputed to have slept here before the battle. (Gupshill Manor has recently undergone extensive structural work and internal refurbishment.) To the walker's left, directly opposite the inn, is a gap in the hedge, through which is Queen Margaret's camp (point C). Although there is little to be seen, it is clear that the site must have commanded a clear view to the south.

Continue along the A38, crossing over to the right-hand side where the footpath continues to the turn-off to Southwick Park, once a prominent residence, and now owned by the local water authority. Walk down the narrow lane to the house. Approaching it, public footpath signs can be seen pointing to the left and right. Walk to the right, in front of the house and then around the perimeter of the playing field to the far corner of the wooded area over to the left, where a narrow track leads through to a single-track road.

Bloody Meadow, where many fleeing Lancastrians were cut down

Follow this road, bearing to the left, and eventually it ends in a T-junction. To the left is Tewkesbury Park Golf and Country Club. Across the road, to the right, is Bloody Meadow (point D), where many fleeing Lancastrians were cut to pieces. Walk over the road and through the gate into the field, where a plan of the battle will be found (Pathfinder 1042 897318). Walk through the field, emerging on to Lower Lode Lane. Turn right and walk back up to Gloucester Road. Cross the road and follow the river through The Vineyards to emerge on to Gander Lane at the rear of the abbey. The Vineyards is sometimes said to be an unlikely spot for Somerset to have chosen to make a stand forming, as it does, part of a deep hollow. But history throws up many examples of poorly-chosen positions, the inadequacies of which are amply demonstrated with the benefit of hindsight. The commander on the spot acting under pressure, may well have been influenced by factors unknown to present-day critics.

# Further Explorations

Tewkesbury has more than its share of fine, timbered houses, but is not quite so picturesque as other Cotswold towns, having a strong industrial base in such diverse trades as grain mills, brewing, stocking manufacture and boot and shoemaking.

To the north-west of the town is the village of Bushley (Pathfinder 1042 874340), where Payne's Place (marked on the map) is situated. Built around 1460, the house is reputed to be the spot where Queen Margaret, having escaped from the battle, spent one of her final nights of freedom. Margaret had placed herself in the care of two monks who guided her across the Severn at Upper Lode (Pathfinder 1042 883331). The owner of Payne's Place, Thomas Payne, a merchant, offered her shelter for the night and the room in which she stayed is still referred to as 'The Queen's Room'. Another house, Owlpen Manor House (Landranger 162 7998), near Dursley, was also visited by the queen en route to Tewkesbury.

# Further Information

Tewkesbury is well appointed as far as the motorist is concerned, junction 9 on the M5 and junction 1 on the M50 linking up with arterial roads through the town. Car-parking can be a problem in the tourist season – particularly on market days (Wednesdays and Saturdays). The best parking is by the abbey, in Gander Lane, looking out over The Vineyards.

It is sometimes claimed that Tewkesbury failed to benefit fully from the Industrial Revolution because it was bypassed by the railway. In fact, Tewkesbury was well served by the railway, notably via the West Midlands–Gloucester line. Unfortunately, this is no longer the case and Gloucester is the most convenient destination, with services from both Paddington and Birmingham. For further details call (0452) 529501. For details of National Express coach services call (0242) 584111. For details of bus services between Gloucester and Tewkesbury, telephone the Tourist Office (see below).

The Tourist Office can be easily reached by turning right into Church Street, continuing to bear right into Barton Street. It is as well to telephone before travelling any distance to ensure that the office and museum will be open (tel: (0684) 295027).

Relevant Ordnance Survey maps for the area are Landrangers 150 and 162, and Pathfinder 1042. Further reading is furnished by P.W. Hammond's *The Battles of Barnet and Tewkesbury* (Alan Sutton Publishing, 1990). The Borough Council has produced a battlefield trail. A leaflet can be picked up from the Tourist Office. It limits itself largely to The Vineyards and Bloody Meadow, although an extension to the public footpath system to accommodate the trail has led to improved access to the latter site.

# 6
# THE BATTLE OF BOSWORTH
## 22 August 1485

## *The Road to Bosworth*

Twelve months prior to the Battle of Bosworth, it seemed impossible that Richard III's position could be seriously threatened. Having acceded in 1483, Richard, Edward IV's brother and the former Duke of Gloucester, had quickly filled most positions of influence with his closest friends and supporters. As it happened, this proved to be a mistake (one which his successor, Henry VII was not to repeat), antagonizing further those whose lands and livelihoods had been confiscated in the process. The fact that the usurpers were northerners did nothing to inspire affection in the hearts of either the south-east or West-Country folk. Richard may have believed that those who had been liberally rewarded for their loyalty would consequently have most to lose in the event of a Lancastrian backlash, and so would prove staunch allies should events necessitate it.

The problem for Richard's beneficiaries lay in gauging the extent to which their master could be trusted. Had he not played with consummate ease the role of friend to Hastings, Clarence, Buckingham – and even Edward and Richard, the young princes in the Tower? The age of chivalry was past, replaced with a regime of duplicity and courtly intrigue. Each man had his price and looked to the cause which best served his own interests and advancement.

As news of the planned invasion by Henry Tudor, the Earl of Richmond, who had been living in exile in Brittany for many years filtered through to the royal courts, Richard took himself to the castle at Nottingham, a geographically central point from which he could counter Henry's preliminary moves. Denouncing his self-exiled enemies, John de Vere, Earl of Oxford and Jasper Tudor, Earl of Pembroke, whose hopes for a come-back were focused on Henry, Richard cajoled and bullied (mostly the latter) a substantial Yorkist army into action.

If Richard found difficulty in recruiting troops, how much greater, then, was Henry's problem, heavily dependent as he was on foreign mercenaries and the charity of the French court? Finally ready to sail on 1 August 1485, his strategy involved playing on his Welsh roots by effecting a landing in Wales. Via his intelligence network, Richard seems to have been aware of this possibility, but there were several likely landing places dotted around the English and Welsh coastlines and it was impossible to establish defensive positions at all of them.

On 7 August 1485, Henry landed at Milford Haven, quite unchallenged, although a trail of beacons did flash a warning. Behaving in a monarchical manner, with much recourse to the royal 'We' in both conversation and correspondence, he remained unsure of the extent of his potential support. Would pledges made while he languished in France be honoured now that the day of reckoning was at hand? At first, it seemed uncertain. As the Pretender moved further inland, his destination Shrewsbury, armed men were gathering, but whether to join or harass him, it was not clear. He did have one major force working in his favour: the centuries-old Celtic hatred of the English. His lack of charisma mattered little for so determined were the Welsh against their old enemies in England, they would have sworn allegiance regardless.

Commitment to the rebel cause gathered momentum, although slowly at first, with only a few recruits or the odd detachment of men donated by wary noblemen, all anxious to display a token support, reluctant to openly declare against the king. Everything therefore depended upon the decisions of men of influence, such as Sir Walter Herbert and Rhys ap Thomas, who finally threw in their lot with Henry, after being promised a share of the spoils of victory.

Richard's response to the news, although swift, was not especially urgent. Uprisings of this nature were rarely successful and it seemed unbecoming for a reigning monarch to give way to panic at every hint of unrest. After all, the struggle between Lancaster and York comprised many years of armed conflict and, at present, Richard was reasonably confident of the stability of his power.

By 17 August, Henry had arrived at Lichfield, while Richard remained immovable at Nottingham, trying vainly to ascertain the strength of the resistance movement. One thing was abundantly clear to the king – he could not depend upon the likes of men such as Thomas, Lord Stanley, who would eventually prove Richard's undoing. Richard had never trusted the Stanleys, whose loyalties traditionally resided with the House of Lancaster. Stanley had refused to commit his men at the Yorkist victory at Blore Heath in 1459, and would do so again at Bosworth. Perhaps Richard foresaw this likelihood for, as the pace on the road to Bosworth quickened, he took the precaution of making a hostage of Stanley's son, Lord Strange. It was, arguably, Stanley and his younger brother, Sir William, however, who were Richard's superiors in the consummate art of perfidy. Thus, while appearing to muster troops for the suppression of the rebellion, they were giving strong moral support to the challenger. The future of the captive Lord Strange looked far from certain.

Mobilization was proving to be a much slower business than Richard had anticipated, and it was not until 20 August that he felt sufficiently confident to march south-west to Leicester, which he reached on the same day. Within twenty-four hours, his force had mushroomed into a vast army. Turning out in support of their king were, among others, the Lords Zouche and Ferrers, the Duke of Norfolk and the Earls of Northumberland, Lincoln, Surrey and Shrewsbury. Richard had the men, therefore, but how was he to set about formulating his battle plans when he did not know whether the Stanleys were for or against him? It was a problem shared, of course, by Henry. Lord Stanley had taken up position at Atherstone on Watling Street, but in what capacity? Was he functioning as the royal vanguard or was he defending the road against the advance of Richard's supporters from the south? Subsequent parleys between Henry and the Stanleyite camp led the Pretender to believe that he could rely on Stanley support, and his preliminary manoeuvres at Bosworth are suggestive of such an agreement.

A view of Ambion Hill from the entrance to the battlefield centre

On 21 August, Richard broke camp, marching out of Leicester, bound for Atherstone. Henry, meanwhile, had decided to take up a position on White Moors – a strange choice of ground, except that a tract of marshland served as a natural line of defence against attack from the north-east. And it was from the north-east that Richard came on – but only as far as the village of Sutton Cheney and the adjoining eminence of Ambion Hill.

# The Battle of Bosworth

The morning of 22 August 1485 dawned with Richard in a seemingly impregnable position. Ambion Hill, rising to a height of 120 ft, bordered by river and marshland to the south and west, was eminently defendable, while his army outnumbered that of the Pretender by at least two thousand men. Richard still could not fathom how Lord Stanley would react, and now the loyalty of the Earl of Northumberland was also giving some cause for concern. The opening phase of the coming battle would be crucial. If Richard were to carry all before him, then there would be no shortage of demonstrative support, but he needed the committed strength of the irresolutes in order to maintain his numerical supremacy and to enable him to implement a battle plan.

By all accounts, the king passed an uncomfortable night, obsessed by visions of Clarence, Hastings and those whose blood he had shed on his long, slippery climb to the throne. He awoke in a bad temper, not improved by missing his breakfast and finding his chaplain unprepared to hold mass. Henry, on the other hand, encamped on White Moors, slept peacefully, had his breakfast and heard mass.

Richard had planned to be on the move earlier than Henry, for by amassing his troops on Ambion Hill, he had fairly hoped to intimidate the opposition and quickly gain the upper hand. Pre-empting this manoeuvre, Henry was busy organizing his own battle lines, his men having little time to gaze in awe at the mighty host they had been sufficiently impetuous to challenge. In the Yorkist vanguard was the Duke of Norfolk, in command of the Royal archers, with Richard's cavalry occupying the second line and the Earl of Northumberland bringing up the rear. With a much smaller force, the mode of Henry's deployment was more or less a foregone conclusion, the rebel army being split into two groups, the larger leading off under the command of the Earl of Oxford, with a smaller contingent, commanded by Henry, following on behind.

It seemed that Henry was hoping that Lord Stanley, who had assumed a position to the south of the Sutton Cheney–Fenny Drayton road, in between the opposing camps, would fill the Lancastrian rearguard vacancy. But Stanley, intent on letting Henry sweat it out refused to commit himself immediately. From White Moors, Henry and Oxford set off up the Sutton Cheney road, rejecting the option of a direct assault from the south-west in favour of a manoeuvre which involved wheeling around before Lord Stanley, and thus, they hoped, drawing him into the fray. It was a bold move for, had Stanley chosen to support Richard, then Henry would have been under attack from both front and rear, and it strongly suggests that something in the nature of a gentlemen's agreement had been reached between Henry and the Stanleys. Methodically, Henry drew up his own troops to Oxford's right, leaving the left flank open for Stanley. At the very least, he would give the impression that he enjoyed his unqualified support. The Stanley response must have been infuriating for both sides, for Lord Thomas withdrew his main body of followers to Dadlington Hill. Certainly, Richard was incensed, ordering the immediate execution of the hostage, Lord Strange. This was never carried out, however, perhaps because his lieutenants, into whose minds some uncertainty as to the outcome of the battle had now crept, had their own futures to consider.

During the course of their preliminary manoeuvres, the rebels may have been subjected to some largely ineffectual artillery fire and some rather more annoying attention from Norfolk's archers. As Oxford led the rebel front lines up the hill, Norfolk charged down to meet him. As it turned out,

After his death on the battlefield, Richard III was mourned by few. Most people, tired of perpetual civil war, wanted only peace and stable government (Royal Collection)

this was an unwise move, for Oxford's response was to dig in, ordering his men to stand firm around their standards. Thus, Oxford had turned the tables, the defenders of a strong position having been transformed into the hard-pressed assailants of the rebel force. In the face of such stubborn resistance and despite cavalry support, the Yorkist line faltered. Richard looked to Northumberland for support, but the earl refused to move – and continued to refuse to move throughout the battle. The Stanleys chose this auspicious moment to throw in their weight, Lord Stanley behind Henry and Sir William from the rear of Ambion Hill – as suspected, on the side of the rebels. And so, Richard played his last card, charging downhill in search of Henry. In the thick of the fighting, his comrades fell at his side one by one. Losing his horse and isolated, Richard fought on, on foot. He may well have called for a horse although, in reality, he no longer had a kingdom to give in exchange. In the end, he fell, hacked to pieces. His crown was handed to Lord Stanley, who placed it on Henry's head.

## The Aftermath

Yorkist casualties are believed to be far greater than Henry's, although estimates vary and one must allow for an element of exaggeration in the accounts of the victors. From an army of around eight thousand men, the Royalists probably lost in the region of a thousand, while Henry's losses may have amounted to a little over a quarter of this figure. With Richard's death, the fighting seemed to draw to a close, the Royalists laying down their arms. There does not appear to have been a very vigorous pursuit of the losers, and these two factors probably kept the casualty figures down to a minimum. Richard's body was stripped of its armour and flung over a horse, in which condition it was taken to Leicester and placed on public view for two days – a disgraceful exhibition, even by the standards of the time – until Henry VII decided it was time to get on with governing his new kingdom.

How did a new ruler, often without previous experience, establish himself in the business of day-to-day government? Perhaps in much the same way as a newly-elected government does today. Daily life in the kingdom went on as before, all within the context of the decaying feudal system, the identity of the party in power mattering little to the man in the street.

Henry's victory did provide opportunity for a little variation, however, and his triumphal march to London took almost a fortnight to accomplish, beset as he was along the way by people anxious to demonstrate their support. A most pressing issue was that of punishment of the vanquished and rewards for the victors. In the matter of the former, Henry, to his credit, saw no reason for punitive measures against the rank and file. The main problem in this respect was how to treat the beaten but surviving leaders. Seven, including Norfolk, Lord Ferrers and Sir Robert Percy, had fallen in battle, considerably decreasing Henry's task. The Earl of Warwick was taken prisoner, while many of Richard's closest friends were deprived of their estates (considerable benefits accruing to the Stanleys). However, the new king did appreciate that he had to balance the necessity of rewarding his supporters with the expediency of placating his erstwhile enemies. Had he been too severe with the surviving Yorkists, he would have been hard pressed to guarantee continuity of government north of the Trent. Thus, staunch Yorkists such as Shrewsbury and Lincoln were spared – at least until such time as the new administration was established.

Two events did much to consolidate Henry's position. Naturally, Charles VIII of France eagerly recognized the new king and, most important of all, there was the symbolic union of the Houses of York and Lancaster with Henry's betrothal to Elizabeth of York, the daughter of Edward IV and Elizabeth Woodville. Thus, far from being vanquished, the House of York was now being invited to enter into an agreement, of sorts, with the House of Lancaster.

Bosworth ranks with Hastings and Naseby as one of the three major battles which have taken place on English soil. All three, within a broad context of continuity, led to fundamental changes in the system of government. Henry VII, who was described by a contemporary as studious rather than learned, had a penchant for paperwork and may fairly be described as the father of modern bureaucracy. And he was to become obsessed with good housekeeping, possession of a healthy personal fortune tempering a monarch's dependency on his counsellors – a lesson a future monarch would have done well to learn.

# The Walk

**Distance:**   5 miles (8 km)

The starting point is Sutton Wharf Bridge (Pathfinder 915 994411) to the south of the battlefield, just under a mile from Sutton Cheney on the Roman road connecting the A447 with the A5. A car-park (point A) for the use of walkers is provided.

Ignoring the inviting, shady path ahead, walk to the road and turn right, over the bridge. Greenhill Farm is to the right where, according to one

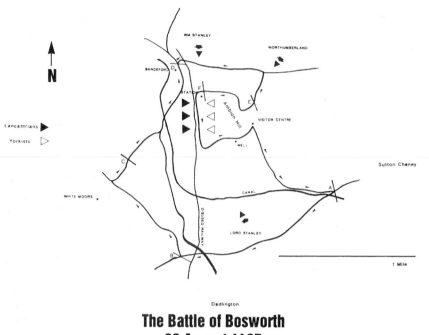

Dadlington

# The Battle of Bosworth
## 22 August 1485

school of thought, Lord Stanley played his waiting game. Beyond the fields lies Ambion Wood, obscuring the view of Ambion Hill.

Walk on and, just beyond the crossroads on the right, there is a public footpath beginning with a stile tucked into the hedgerow (point B). Enter the field and aim for the hedgerow opposite. Here, to the left of centre, there is another stile (which can be obscured during the summer months by the tree which stands before it). Cross over and turn to the left to approach Orchard Farm (Pathfinder 914 395989). Enter the farmyard, where there are vociferous but otherwise harmless dogs, and walk over to the next stile, ahead to the right, and cross over (the tops of the stile posts are painted in yellow to mark the path). Hugging the hedgerow aim for the next path marker, indicating the route across a ploughed field. Aim for the centre of the hedgerow ahead.

Cross into the next field, where the farmer has left the public footpath unploughed, making it easier to follow. White Moors is over to the left as one crosses Henry's line of advance as he marched on Ambion Hill. Coming up on the right is the New Barn group of farm buildings. Drawing level with it, one arrives at a junction. Instead of going straight on turn to the right, towards the farm, following the path around the back of the farmhouse, to emerge on to the wide track leading to the farm (point C).

The battlefield trail signs are starting to appear and these are a great help in keeping you on the straight and narrow. Reaching the road at the end of the track, turn to the left. Walking up the road, with the Lodge on the left, one will once again be in the line of advance of Henry's army. Take care crossing the narrow bridge spanning the canal, and shortly after passing Shenton station, there is a well-marked path leading into King Richard's Field, and the scene of Richard's death (point D).

Return to the road and at the junction opposite the field, turn right under the railway bridge (Pathfinder 893 396007) in the direction of Sutton Cheney. Having cleared the bridge, Ambion Hill becomes visible, looming up on the right, and only at this vantage point can one appreciate the strength of Richard's chosen site. The fields have only a slight gradient as they fan out from the road, before rising sharply. To the left is the ground where Sir William Stanley waited. Although refusing to risk an attack, as soon as Richard disappeared from view in a desperate assault on Henry's position, Stanley took his chance, perhaps secure in the knowledge that he could depend upon Northumberland's inactivity.

Continue to the entrance of the battlefield centre to the right. Walk in and up towards the centre. Near the top (point E) look to the right, for a path (untidy and curiously unmarked) leading across the ridge of the hill. This track becomes very well defined, leading around to the right, hugging the hedgerow. At short intervals, the path is decorated with plaques, delineating aspects of the battle, for the battlefield trail now being followed is provided for the benefit of tourists.

For a while, the walk takes on the aspect of a tour of a stately home. (At the height of the tourist season, it can get exceptionally busy.) The path goes down towards Shenton station (point F), with a view across to Sandeford (the name by which Richard's Field is known). Walk into the station courtyard and, turning to the left, continue to follow the battlefield trail along the disused railway embankment. This is a straight path which, again, has various plaques sited at strategic points along the way, and takes one through the site of fierce fighting between the Earl of Oxford and the Duke of Norfolk.

At the end of the path, enter the gate on the left, to follow the northern margin of Ambion Wood. It is hard to believe that, at the time of the battle, this area was marshland. A little further on, however, it becomes easier to appreciate as, in wet weather, the path becomes quite boggy in parts. Continue to King Richard's Well (Pathfinder 915 402999), a monument erected in the early nineteenth century and lovingly restored by the Richard III Society in 1964.

The battlefield centre car-park is now in view and, beyond this, the battlefield centre complex of gift shops and cafeteria. Prior to the creation of the battlefield centre and trail, walkers were very often discouraged from

Ambion Hill from the direction of Sir William Stanley's line of advance

encroaching on the site, whereas today, it is open to all. Bosworth battlefield is quite rightly regarded as a showpiece among battlefields, a shining example of what can be done to both create and preserve an environment which encourages the appreciation of an event of immense historical significance.

After taking refreshment, if required, turn left on leaving the complex, and strike out through the gate and across the fields for Ambion Wood. The path (again, possibly quite boggy) leads through the wood and down to the Ashby de la Zouch Canal. Follow the path to the left, along the canal bank, leading back to the starting point at Sutton Wharf Bridge.

# Further Explorations

Turning into the approach road to the battlefield centre, one may have noticed a 'Battlefield Church' sign, pointing in the direction of Sutton Cheney. It was at Sutton Cheney church (Pathfinder 894 005417) that Richard heard his last mass. The church, which is open to visitors, contains a memorial brass (erected in 1967) to Richard and all who fell in the battle, and is well worth visiting.

Kirby Muxloe (Landranger 140 5204) was the home of Lord Hastings (executed by Richard in 1483), who converted it from an existing manor-house, which had once belonged to the Earl of Ormonde, who had been beheaded after Towton. All that remains of this once imposing structure is a little low walling and parts of the gatehouse and north-west corner tower.

Kirby Muxloe has now been swallowed up by Leicester, and the city itself is of interest. The West Bridge, by which Richard led his army towards Bosworth, bears a plaque recording a curious prophecy. A fifteenth-century psychic, having been asked to predict the result of the coming battle, announced that wherever Richard's spur struck, his head would be broken. A stone of some height stood upon Bow Bridge and, as chance would have it, Richard struck his spur against it. When his body was brought back to the city, slung over a saddle, his head smashed against the same stone.

Leicester was once well known for its religious institutions. One of these – a hospital – was begun by Henry of Lancaster in 1330. In due course, the premises were extended and a church (or 'new-work') was added – hence the surviving name of the thoroughfare bordering the complex, The Newarke. Lord Hastings took a considerable interest in the development of this foundation, and it was in The Newarke church that Richard's body lay exposed to public scrutiny.

# Further Information

Bosworth battlefield is not an easy place to reach. By road, the best approach is by the A5, Watling Street, branching off just south of Atherstone, via Fenny Drayton.

The approach by rail has possibilities for the railway enthusiast. Hinckley, as well as Leicester, is served by British Rail (tel: (0533) 629811). If one is lucky it is possible to catch the steam train from Market Bosworth to Shenton station on the Shackerstone to Shenton Light Railway. From Leicester, one can reach Market Bosworth by bus. Telephone Leicester Tourist Office (0533 511300) for details of all bus services. However, to coordinate an Inter-City journey with the bus and the limited light railway timetable requires careful planning. To obtain the full benefit of a visit to the area, a weekend stay is recommended – try the Nuneaton Crest Motel (tel: (0203) 5335) on Watling Street (Landranger 140 3993).

Most of the information one might desire about the Battle of Bosworth, including details of facilities and opening times, should come from the battlefield warden, who actually lives on site, at the battlefield centre (tel: (0455) 292239).

Relevant Ordnance Survey maps are Landranger 140 and Pathfinders 893, 894, 914, and 915, the battlefield being cunningly split into almost equal map quarters. Further, and essential, reading is *The Battle of Bosworth* by Michael Bennett (Alan Sutton Publishing, 1985).

# 7
# THE BATTLE OF STOKE FIELD
## 16 June 1487

## *The Road to Stoke Field*

The last of the Plantagenets was Edward, Earl of Warwick, the son of the late Duke of Clarence, and his continued existence, albeit as a prisoner, necessarily posed a threat in terms of his capacity as a potential Yorkist rallying point. There was, of course, the mystery of the princes in the Tower although, oddly enough, the death of the unfortunate pair was an accepted fact in fifteenth-century England. That they were murdered on the orders of Richard III is possible, and, although Richard's supporters today claim that he had no connection with the affair, it is true that he had much to gain (and did gain) by their removal from public life. Had the pair still lived in 1485, it is unlikely that Henry would have been sufficiently confident to launch his invasion, and thereby take the crown.

After Bosworth, therefore, when surviving Yorkists were searching for a focal point for their cause, it was decided to sponsor someone to impersonate Edward whom they knew to be still alive. The wretch duly selected was one Lambert Simnel, the ten-year-old son of an Oxford tradesman, whose claim was effectively managed by Richard Simons, a priest with an eye for the main chance. According to Simons' persuasive argument, Simnel was none other than Edward who had escaped from the Tower. Simons took his protégé across the sea to Ireland where on 24 May 1487, the claimant was actually crowned Edward VI.

The ruse put Henry in a difficult position. He knew that this claimant was an imposter, but could he afford to prove it by bringing the real Edward out into the open? By the time he had decided to do so, it was too late, as the revolt was gathering momentum under the executive direction of the Earl of Lincoln.

Lincoln had been named by Richard III as heir apparent, in preference to Edward, and, contemptuous of Henry's pardon, Lincoln used Simnel as a front for furthering his own advancement. As Richard's nominated heir,

Lincoln could have made his own bid for the throne, so, in some respects, Simnel's claim was superfluous to the Yorkist cause. To confuse matters even further Edward, whom Simnel was impersonating, had a good claim to the throne in his own right. Lincoln's sudden flight to the Netherlands in March 1487 left Henry quite perplexed as to planning, and what his own course of action should be.

Unclear as to the direction from which any invasion might come, Henry decided to base himself, temporarily at least, at Coventry. Even before he had reached his destination, an invasion fleet, consisting of German mercenaries and led by Lincoln, Lord Lovel and other exiles, was setting sail for the Irish coast. Ireland under the tutelage of the Fitzgeralds, had always been fiercely Yorkist in sentiment. Sir Thomas Fitzgerald, the Chancellor of Ireland, and his brother, the Earl of Kildare, did their best to drum up support for the Pretender and it was Fitzgerald who joined the invasion force at the head of a mix of Scots mercenaries and Irish infantry.

On 4 June 1487, Lincoln and his party, including Simnel, landed on the Lancashire coast, to be welcomed by the prominent local Yorkist, Sir Thomas Broughton. Slowly at first, and then more rapidly, the army made its way inland. On 8 June, gathering momentum and adherents, it reached Masham, where further efforts on its behalf were made by the Lords Scrope. The preliminary rebel objective was York, but messengers dispatched to the city found its leading citizens lukewarm in their response. Having applied themselves to adapting to the realities of Tudor rule, they were not convinced that their best interests would be served by supporting a rag-bag rebellion. The rebels were advised that the gates would be closed to them. Simultaneously, letters were sent to Henry from York, apprising him of the situation and asking for speedy assistance. Clearly, to lay siege to the city was out of the question when speed was of the essence. Accordingly, Lincoln pressed on to Boroughbridge to join the Great North Road.

Meanwhile, Henry had not been idle. As the rebel army moved south, he marched to Leicester where he paused, making efforts to determine the degree of re-awakened popular Yorkist support. From Leicester, he marched to Nottingham, where he was reinforced by George Stanley, Lord Strange. When Henry left Nottingham, the two armies were on a collision course which seemed likely to lead to a head-on clash at Newark.

# The Battle of Stoke Field

As Newark occupies such a prominent position in terms of north–south communications, sited on the River Trent at the intersection of the Great

North Road and the Fosse Way, it is difficult to understand why the town has not developed beyond its twenty-five thousand inhabitants. Certainly, between the twelfth and seventeenth centuries, throughout the years of internal strife, the town's strategic position endowed it with an importance equal, if not superior, to that of neighbours with a loftier pedigree, such as Lincoln or Nottingham.

Newark profited in times of peace but also stood to lose in times of war. Having come through the Wars of the Roses virtually unscathed, it now seemed a particularly cruel twist of fate that the town should have to host a major battle for, by mid-June, it was abundantly clear that the town stood in the way of two advancing armies – Henry marching from the south-west and the rebels descending from the north-west. On 15 June, the rebels crossed the Trent at Fiskerton, pitching their tents around the village of East Stoke. Henry, meanwhile, was encamped 6 miles to the south, at Radcliffe.

On this occasion, it was the rebels who had the advantage of choice of ground. The high ground, known as Burham Furlong, immediately to the south-west of East Stoke (much to the relief of the good citizens of Newark, no doubt), seemed as good as any. The only problem was how best to deploy the rebel force. This was more difficult than might at first be imagined because although the rebel camp boasted such eminent leaders as Lovel, Fitzgerald, Sir Thomas Broughton and Lincoln himself, there was not one among them with a record of field command. For strategic planning, therefore, much responsibility rested upon the broad shoulders of the German mercenary, Colonel Schwartz.

The colonel had little option but to hold them together as a single fighting unit. Even this presented difficulties, for the only dependable element comprised the mercenaries themselves. The Irish contingent, barefoot, lightly armed and undisciplined, was likely to prove hard to manage, while the commitment of the newly recruited English would, as always, be open to question. And so it was decided that the army should be drawn up on Burham Furlong, the mercenaries in the front line, with the precious little cavalry covering each wing. The Irish would be placed a little apart to be introduced as added weight, as and when it was considered necessary.

Henry started 16 June in much the same way that he had started 22 August two years before, at Bosworth, by hearing mass. From Radcliffe, he then set out along the Fosse Way, the sight of the orderly advance of his well-armed host, outnumbering them by two to one, doing little to bolster the confidence of the rebels – particularly as their own figurehead, Simnel, was hardly of an age to deliver rallying speeches to the troops.

The Royal vanguard, its flanks protected by cavalry, and commanded by the Earl of Oxford – who had done so much to ensure victory at Bosworth – advanced on the rebel positions, Henry following, with Lord Strange bringing up the rear. Although the rebel mercenaries included crossbowmen among their number, Oxford's vanguard was resplendent with English longbows and wave after wave of steel-tipped arrows wrought fearful havoc in the tightly-packed rebel ranks. Perceiving that there was little chance of Oxford trying to take the hill when he could so decimate the defenders at long-range, Lincoln decided, as Richard had done at Bosworth, to take the fight to the enemy in one death-defying assault. Gathering momentum, the rebels charged, *en masse*, into Oxford's front line, sending a shock wave throughout the vanguard. Less seasoned troops would have given way, but although the royal line sagged, it showed no sign of collapse.

During this critical stage of the battle, Henry kept a wary eye to his rear and to Lord Strange, the craftiness of the Stanleys uppermost in his thoughts. Then, choosing his moment carefully, he threw his weight in behind Oxford, who, thus reinforced, began to push the rebels back up the hill. The Irish, who had been expecting an easy victory, fell prey to the renewed vigour of the Royalist assault. While the mercenaries closed ranks and fought on to the end, the rest of Lincoln's army scattered in the direction of the Trent. Many were cut off in a ravine running down to the river, which henceforth took the name of 'Red Gutter' as a result of the carnage which took place there. The Royalist victory was complete.

## *The Aftermath*

By the standards of the time, casualties were high. Henry probably lost upwards of a thousand men, while the rebel dead amounted to at least four times that number. Simnel was taken prisoner, although his campaign leaders, Lincoln, Fitzgerald and Martin Schwartz, all chose a soldier's death rather than risk falling into the king's vengeful hands. The fate of Viscount Lovel is less certain as he disappeared without trace. Henry, anxious to prove that he was in fact dead, granted Lovel's wife, Anna, a widow's pension. As he was last seen struggling across the Trent, it is probable that Lovel did, in fact, drown. However, there subsequently developed a legend to the effect that he had somehow survived the victorious army's pursuit, to take refuge in his home, Minster Lovell, in Oxfordshire, where he spent the rest of a miserable life in hiding. Perhaps the story is more than mere legend for, over two centuries later, when building work was being carried out at Minster Lovell, a secret underground chamber was discovered and, with it, a human skeleton, seated before a table, as if in the act of writing. Were these the remains of Francis Lovel, who, by some accident to a confederate, had been abandoned to a terrible death?

The king himself, keen to put as much distance as possible between

After the Battle of Stoke Field, Henry VII displayed his contempt for the symbol of Yorkist hopes, Lambert Simnel, by putting him to work as a scullion in the royal kitchen (Hulton Deutsch)

himself and the bloody battlefield, repaired to Newark, where he conferred sundry titles on those who had distinguished themselves in the fighting. From Newark, he travelled to Lincoln where the festivities continued apace. In truth, Henry needed to keep his army together for a few days longer until he could be sure that what remained of the rebel contingent could be rounded up and dealt with. And so, the dead were buried, while the survivors, with protestations of loyalty to their sovereign, returned to their homes.

The figurehead of the Yorkist challenge, Lambert Simnel, was treated with measured contempt, being assigned to the royal kitchens. His erstwhile tutor, Simons, was sentenced to life imprisonment. In all, the Simnel affair has a distinctly low-key flavour, and this is because Henry tried to play down its importance. In reality, the victory at Stoke Field consolidated Henry's success at Bosworth. Stoke was a battle waiting to happen, the opportunity needed by the new administration to flex its muscles, to demonstrate to the country at large and, even more important, to the European powers, that it was here to stay.

The serious view that Henry took of the revolt is exemplified by the indecent haste with which he now organized an event he had constantly deferred – the coronation of his queen, Elizabeth of York. The grand occasion was set for November of that year as a further demonstration of unity between Lancaster and York, even though Henry's heart was not really in it. He declined to take an active part in the ceremony, choosing instead to watch it as a spectator.

# *The Walk*

**Distance:**   6 miles (9½ km)

In some ways, it is a good idea to visit any battlefield on the anniversary of the battle. One at least stands a chance of being able to appreciate the conditions in which the armies fought – although it also means that enthusiasts are more likely to be out in force. As Stoke Field occurred on 18 June, then a sunny summer afternoon may be the best time for a visit.

When searching for a suitable starting point for a walk, it is best to begin some distance from the battlefield centre. In this way, the preliminary moves

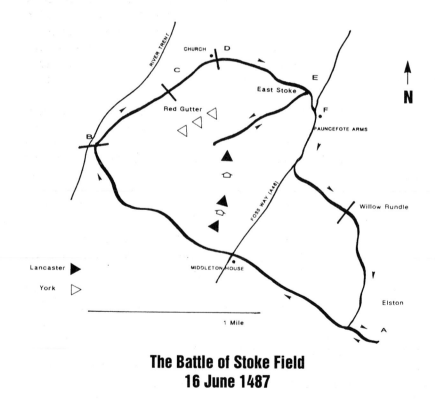

## The Battle of Stoke Field
## 16 June 1487

of the opposing forces can be absorbed into the itinerary. Therefore, this walk commences in the village of Elston. There is parking on Lodge Lane, opposite the church (Pathfinder 813 758479) (point A). Walk along Lodge Lane towards the A46. The road runs past The Hall and, at the corner of Lodge Lane and the A46, is Middleton House (Pathfinder 813 747486), a Victorian edifice looking curiously out of place in a rural landscape, but which acts as an excellent landmark.

With care, cross the A46 and head for the farm track, directly opposite Lodge Lane. Enter by the gate and continue straight ahead. The Royalist vanguard under the Earl of Oxford would have moved across the path from left to right, while the remainder of the royal army lagged well behind along the Fosse Way. Continue along the track to be rewarded with a splendid view of the River Trent. As it approaches the river, the path peters out. When it seems that one can proceed no further, turn into the field to the left and walk along the hedgerow towards the river. A stile (point B) at the end of the field enables one to gain the footpath following the river bank, which is crumbling in parts, so a little care may be necessary.

One may be forgiven for supposing that the area is not frequented by ramblers, for the path is often lost in bracken. Keep close to the river bank to avoid going wrong. Lincoln deployed his Yorkist troops on the high ground to the right. Further on, also to the right, Stoke Wood (Pathfinder 813 742497) looms up. Between the wood and the river bank, a bridle-way runs across the fields. On reaching a sign which says 'Gas Pipelines', turn inland towards the wood to see the bridle-way marked with a footpath arrow.

Step out on the path, which veers gently towards the wood. Just before it widens out into a farm track, approaching a rusty iron gate (point C), one may discern Red Gutter running up through the wood. Walk around the gate (which will probably disintegrate if any attempt is made to open it) and out on to the road. To the left is the road to Fiskerton, the route the Yorkists took to reach Stoke Field. Walk straight on and, on a sharp right-hand bend, St Oswald's church will come into view. Enter the churchyard (Pathfinder 796 748501) at the gate just before the overhead footbridge (point D).

One of life's little pleasures is exploring a church on a weekday when it is deserted. On the left, on entering, is a pair of new doors, leading up to the bell tower. Resisting the temptation to indulge in a little campanology, walk over to the far wall to examine some publicity material relevant to the battlefield. In 1987, for the quincentenary of the battle, Nottinghamshire County Council made an effort to create a battlefield trail. Unfortunately, it has never caught the public imagination in the same way as Bosworth, and is now abandoned and almost impossible to find.

On leaving the church, note that the churchyard itself is rather high when compared with the surrounding area. It has been suggested that the present

A view of the battlefield from the Fosse Way, looking up towards the Yorkist positions before Stoke Wood

yard overlies a much earlier one, the level of which was filled as a result of mass burials occasioned by the battle. Keen observers may also note the battered stonework at the entrance to the church due, it is claimed, to the sharpening of swords prior to the conflict.

Continue along the main road towards East Stoke. In the village, turn down Humber Lane (point E) to the right. Take the rough track between the houses and the school. To the left is the spot where Oxford was hotly engaged by Lincoln and the German mercenaries. Momentarily, it seemed that the Yorkists had the upper hand, but then the main body of Henry's army swept up from the Fosse Way and turned the tide in the royal favour. The poorly-armed Irish, having eagerly joined the fray in the hope of being in at the kill, actually found themselves bearing the brunt of the counter-attack. Breaking ranks, they retreated down towards the river, many getting no further than Red Gutter, where they were slaughtered by their pursuers.

Humber Lane peters out a little way past Stoke Wood, so return to the village, turning right towards the Fosse Way. Cross the road carefully to walk along the hard footpath back towards Elston. (Refreshments are available, if required, at the Pauncefote Arms (point F).) Continue to Elston Lane and turn left along Elston Lane, the starting position of the Irish contingent of the rebel army. A little way past the white bungalow, at the side of the road to the right, is what I have always taken to be the Willow Rundle (Pathfinder 813 755489), a water trough, marking the spot where a certain combatant in the battle fell. Before he died, he told his companions that if he went to heaven, a spring would appear to flow in perpetuity. A spring, which never dries up and which never freezes over, did appear, from which one may safely presume that the soldier's soul rests in peace.

At Elston (surely one of the prettiest villages in England) turn left down Pinfold Lane. At the end, turn left back on to Lodge Lane. Continue walking past the Hall to the church and starting point.

# *Further Explorations*

A little to the north of East Stoke is the site of a Roman fort, *Ad Pontem* (Pathfinder 796 759504), providing evidence of three hundred years of Roman occupation – hardly surprising, taking into account its position on the Fosse Way. From time to time, coins and pottery are discovered. It is also likely that the area, as part of a subjugated Mercia was overrun and pillaged by the Danes.

In the early middle ages, the land on which the battle was fought was owned by a family which took the name de Stoke and Courts Baron were held at East Stoke for over four hundred years. In the early thirteenth century, the de Stokes established a public right of way to the ferry crossing to Fiskerton, and this track exists today, beginning at the rear of Stoke Wood (Pathfinder 813 743499) and terminating at the Trent (Pathfinder 796 740509).

The original manor-house of the village stood on the site presently occupied by the Hall (Pathfinder 796 749501). Another building which once occupied this site was the medieval Hospital of Saint Leonard, founded in the mid-twelfth century. Its patron at the time of the Battle of Stoke Field was Lord Lovel – a position subsequently taken by the Crown in the person of Henry VII. The hospital was closed by Queen Elizabeth I.

The Ordnance Pathfinder map 813 suggests many possibilities for further exploration in the area. At Sibthorpe (762455) there is a medieval dovecote, which is well worth seeing. The map also indicates a roadway (762460) called Deadwrong Lane, a walk along which allows one time to ponder on how it may have come about its name. Running almost the full length of the right-hand side of the map is a disused railway, which is certainly worth a stroll. Elston itself has a windmill (761477) and ruined chapel (762483).

Unmarked on the map is Dead Man's Field, to the north of East Stoke (Pathfinder 796 759502) – perhaps a grim indication of the true resting place of the battlefield dead.

# Further Information

East Stoke is probably one of the most accessible – perhaps *the* most accessible – of British battlefields. Located in the heart of England and adjacent to Newark, it can be reached by both road and rail. By road, the battlefield is approached via the Fosse Way – the A46 Leicester to Grimsby trunk road, which runs through East Stoke. Elston is directly off the A46 just to the south of East Stoke.

For British Rail services, telephone (0636) 704491. For National Express coach services, telephone (0602) 585317. There are bus stops both in East Stoke (by the Pauncefote Arms) and by the junction of the A46 and Lodge Lane. For local services, contact Lincolnshire Road Car Co. Ltd (tel: (0636) 702173).

The Tourist Office at Newark can be contacted on (0636) 78962.

Ordnance Survey maps Landranger 129 and Pathfinders 813 and 796 refer. Essential reading is provided by *Lambert Simnel and the Battle of Stoke* by Michael Bennett (Alan Sutton Publishing, 1987).

# INTRODUCTION

The English Civil War differs from earlier wars which had taken place on English soil, all of which had amounted to little more than baronial struggles. It was certainly not a class conflict, as so often claimed, for many of the nobility fought against the king while the rural peasantry often remained stoically conservative. So, how did a country which had, in large measure, enjoyed internal peace for over one hundred and fifty years find itself engaged in a bloody six-year struggle which set father against son, brother against brother, and which culminated, in 1649, in regicide?

Charles I's reign had opened in 1625 with a war, against the old enemy, Spain. The new king had been a backward child, unable to speak through some deformity until he was five, and he relied heavily on his friend, the Duke of Buckingham, for counsel. Buckingham was an adventurer and, not content with waging war against Spain, he also plunged the country into a war with the French, compelling his master to call Parliament with a view to obtaining funds.

The law did not oblige the king to call Parliament. Provided he was able to manage on his combined income from Crown lands, customs duties and feudal dues, there was no reason to do so. But, whenever there was a need for additional taxation, Parliament had to give its approval. Successive Parliaments, called by Charles to approve measures for financing hostilities with France and Spain, provided his enemies within the House with opportunities to impose conditions geared to compromising his 'Divine Right' to rule. It is likely that matters would have come to a head much earlier than 1642, had not Buckingham been assassinated. Deprived of his adviser, Charles learned to stand alone and, accordingly, became much more assertive where Parliamentary demands were concerned. In due course, Thomas Wentworth, subsequently the Earl of Strafford, took over Buckingham's role. Although hot-tempered, he seemed well-suited to keeping the peace, believing, as he did, in the unity of king and Parliament.

However, the essentially Presbyterian Parliament also feared that Charles was a concealed 'papist', who favoured a return to the Church of Rome. His appointment of William Laud as Archbishop of Canterbury aroused much Parliamentary hostility. Although Laud entertained no popish sympathies, he did preach the duty of obedience and adherence to the principle of 'Divine Right'. Among his innovations were the railing-off of the altar and a new emphasis on ceremony and the dignity of the clergy. The gulf between clergy and congregation was therefore widened in more than one sense of the word, much to the chagrin of the dissenting Puritans.

With the conclusion of the French and Spanish wars, England embarked on a period of peace, although internal strife continued to grow apace, with Charles's attempts to impose new taxation without recourse to Parliamentary approval. The most unpopular of these taxes was the infamous 'ship money', raised in 1634. Proceeds went directly to the Navy for the maintenance of a peace-time fleet. Although, arguably, Charles acted within the law to impose it on coastal districts, it was extended a year later to cover the whole country. This resulted in a Puritanical revolt led by John Hampden, who challenged the king's right to create what was, he claimed, a brand new tax, without convening and consulting Parliament. This opposition was so well orchestrated as to render the tax virtually uncollectable.

At the same time, serious problems were brewing within the Church, as Archbishop Laud proposed introducing a new Anglican prayer-book in Scotland. Charles had little understanding of the Scots – he had visited Scotland only once – and in 1637, without consulting the Scottish Parliament, he ordered the use of the prayer-book north of the border. Not surprisingly, it was rejected by the Kirk (the Church of Scotland), and it became clear that the king would have to fight if he wished to be obeyed. In the spring of 1640, he called Parliament to plead for financial backing to raise an army. The Chamber, led by John Pym, refused and, dependent upon his own feeble resources, the best Charles could do was to conjure up a provincial militia, which the Scots soon overran, occupying the counties of Durham and Northumberland. Charles was left with no choice but to recall Parliament.

Pym and his supporters had Charles with his back to the wall – and they knew it. Both Strafford and Laud were arrested. The latter was executed after languishing in the Tower for eight long years, but Strafford went to the block within twelve months on a trumped-up charge of treason, Charles allowing himself to be manipulated into signing the death warrant. This was the turning point, for the king's weakness in sacrificing his friend gave Pym *carte blanche* to behave as he pleased. All taxes levied without Parliamentary authority, including ship money, were declared illegal, while the Triennial Act bound the sovereign to call Parliament every three years. There followed demands that Parliament should endorse selection of the royal Ministers and that the Church of England should be Presbyterianized. All this and more, Charles approved without resistance. Pym must have wondered what he had to do to goad

Charles into making a rash move. Playing his final card, in January 1642, Pym proposed impeaching the queen.

This was, indeed, to have the desired result for, on 4 January 1642, Charles arrived in person at the House of Commons to arrest, among others, Pym and Hampden, on charges of treason. Accompanied by between three and four hundred Cavaliers, he burst into the Chamber only to find, in his own words, that 'the birds are flown'. Perhaps already aware of the error he had committed in forcing his way into the Chamber, he withdrew in some embarrassment.

News of the failed coup spread rapidly through the London streets and a mob was soon besieging the palace, causing the royal family to flee westwards to Hampton Court. Pym, meanwhile, made a triumphal return to the House. When Charles next entered the capital, it was to stand trial for his life. By stages, the king withdrew to Newmarket, Nottingham and York, slowly gathering support and joined by his nephew, Prince Rupert of the Palatinate, an experienced soldier, while last-ditch negotiations to avert the approaching conflict continued. When these failed, Robert Devereux, the Earl of Essex, was authorized to command a Parliamentary army. On 22 August 1642, the Royal Standard was raised at Nottingham. A light breeze blew it to the ground.

# *Warfare in the English Civil War*

By the time of the English Civil War in the 1640s, armour had become much more refined. Freedom of movement and speed of action were the order of the day, a man's armour often comprising only a helmet and breastplate. Musketeers wore no armour at all. Although it offered no protection against bullets, leather was often preferred to metal by cavalry. An exception to the rule was made by the few cuirassier regiments, which were encased in armour from head to knee. In practice, of course, much depended upon availability of materials and the Roundheads, with control of London and the major ports, had the advantage in this respect. Royalist commanders would raise and equip troops at their own expense. In the beginning – at Edgehill, for example – Royalist infantry were often attractively kitted out, which was not the case as the war progressed and personal fortunes dissolved.

Similarly, Parliament held the advantage as far as firearms were concerned. The blade was still paramount, but use of muskets and pistols was on the increase – a trend accelerated by improvements effected during the conflict. Artillery was another matter. The advantage of speed, gained by the decline of heavy body armour, could easily be offset by the burden of a cumbersome artillery train. Heavy guns did not play a decisive field role in the war.

Something which it is easy to ignore is the role played by the Navy during the conflict. As the Battle of Britain is inclined to overshadow the Battle of the Atlantic in accounts of the Second World War, so Prince Rupert's enthralling cavalry charges tend to obscure the significance of the Parliamentary seizure of the English fleet. While Oxford was geographically well placed to act as the hub for Royalist activity, it was no substitute for freedom of movement in and around coastal waters. As Charles came to depend more and more upon continental Europe for war materials, so the Parliamentary blockade began to take its toll. The Royalists, of course, did their best to create a Navy of their own and contrived, with difficulty, to keep open lines of communication between England and Europe, through a fleet of small ships geared to running the blockade from the shelter of the few ports open to Royalist traffic.

Another area in which Parliament outshone the Royalists was in espionage. Charles had not felt in need of a secret service. Had he possessed one in the first instance, perhaps he would have been better informed about what was happening in Parliament and the country at large. As the war progressed, so spies became more active, but whereas the king depended upon informers (usually friends, whose reports were based on optimism rather than on fact), Parliamentary intelligence grew into a well-organized service – to be developed into a political necessity after the war, by Cromwell's spy master, John Thurloe.

In some respects, the Civil War was as much about enforced inactivity as about fierce fighting, with much of the war effort on both sides being concentrated on the laying, withstanding and lifting of sieges. While stories of rape and pillage are an integral part of accounts of several of the major sieges of the war, the real enemy was disease, with typhus followed by plague wreaking havoc among the civilian population. Indeed, it has been claimed that, in relative terms, the death toll of the Civil War was at least equal to that of the First World War.

During the two centuries that had elapsed since the Wars of the Roses, one aspect of warfare remained almost unchanged – the treatment of the wounded. Even those casualties who were fortunate enough to receive the best of medical care had to trust to luck for their survival. In theory, regiments enjoyed the services of surgeons, but in practice the wounded were often abandoned with the dead on the field of battle, either to be finished off or cared for by the local populace.

# 8
# THE BATTLE OF EDGEHILL
## 23 October 1642

## *The Road to Edgehill*

With both king and Parliament issuing rival commands for militia levies, each district was obliged to decide which side to obey, the future of the war depending largely on how sides were taken at the outset. As far as patterns of support can be ascertained, the centres of rebellion were those with grievances – trading towns where taxes had aroused most resentment and where Presbyterianism was strongest: East Anglia, the West Riding and all the chief trading ports. The strongly Royalist areas were those where ties between the gentry and their tenants were still strong – the north, the west and Wales, together with most of the smaller cathedral cities. Clearly, Charles was obliged to press for a quick victory, for the longer the war went on, the stronger Parliament would become with control of both the main centres of trade and the major ports.

Early in September, Essex had amassed an army of some twenty thousand, scattered between Coventry and Northampton and equipped from the magazines at Hull (which had, in April, raised its drawbridges against the king). From a base in Shrewsbury, Charles was still recruiting in the west – and with some success, for his force had grown to some two thousand horse and six thousand foot.

Allowing for relatively minor clashes throughout the country, notably at Hull in July and at Powick Bridge in September, the war was still of a 'phoney' nature and neither side had fully organized or taken advantage of any form of military intelligence. Thus, the Royalists were unaware of Essex's strength while, for his part, Essex had little idea of the king's movements. Therefore, although Charles struck camp at Shrewsbury on 12 October, the Parliamentary army made no attempt to intercept him until a week later.

Logistics were a problem for both armies, which simply collected recruits while on the march. The only realistic method of provisioning was by plunder, in which Royalists and Roundheads alike indulged with impunity. Anxious to consolidate wherever possible, Essex reduced his strength by establishing garrisons in towns such as Banbury and Warwick. Had he not divided his main force in this manner, he would have maintained a numerical supremacy at Edgehill, perhaps sufficient to enable him to end the war at a single blow. With the benefit of hindsight, however, many wars would have been of but brief duration. As it was, with the Royalists gathering strength every day, Essex possessed no accurate estimate of their numbers, and history has been a little unkind in its condemnation of him as over-cautious.

According to the contemporary historian, Sir Edward Hyde, Earl of Clarendon, although both armies were not too far apart and were marching roughly in the same direction, neither side knew the location of the other. On 22 October, the Royalists held a conference at Edgcote, to the north-east of Banbury. Essex, meanwhile, had reached Kineton, only 12 miles away to the west. At this time, arranging accommodation for armies was as big a problem as provisioning them, and troops could be scattered around for miles. As it was, both Royalists and Roundheads planned to use Wormleighton, midway between Edgcote and Kineton, and it was not until troops ran into each other in the village that either side became aware of the other's proximity.

Rupert supported the notion of attacking the enemy immediately, counting on surprise to overwhelm the opposition. Another option was to make a run for it, in the hope that the king would reach London first. In the end, something of a compromise was reached, whereby the Royalists would stand and fight, taking up a position on the brow of Edgehill, an eminently respectable choice. Thus, the morning of 23 October found the king's army awaiting Essex, who was hastily marshalling his men into battle order on the plain beneath. By this time, both armies numbered about fourteen thousand men; by nightfall, fifteen hundred would be dead.

## The Battle of Edgehill

One wonders who was most surprised, the Parliamentarians upon seeing the Royalists leave their vantage point, or the Royalists when Essex allowed them to descend to the plain unmolested. One thing is certain – the Parliamentarians were the first to open fire, with volleys directed towards the king and his easily identifiable entourage. Charles's aides had difficulty in persuading him to withdraw to a safe position. He fully intended to march

The Battle of Edgehill

with his army. Eventually, he retired to the high ground that still bears the name Bullet Hill, although even here, he still presented a fair target for the big guns of his enemies.

The Parliamentarians may have fired the first shots, but the Royalists commenced battle proper with spectacular cavalry charges. As Prince Rupert advanced on the right, Parliamentarian cannon-balls flew harmlessly over his horsemen's heads. A musket volley discharged before the Royalist horse was in range similarly did little damage. The sight of the Cavalier charge gathering momentum proved too much for Sir James Ramsay's horse and they turned tail, being mercilessly pursued by the Royalists, who swept on to Kineton where the opposition's baggage train was plundered.

Meanwhile, on the left flank, Lord Wilmot was enjoying similar success. He had a more difficult task, advancing over rough ground, over hedges and through ditches lined with musketeers. Yet, the Cavaliers again carried all before them and Colonel Richard Fielding's Parliamentarians were contemptuously brushed aside. Wilmot was only marginally more successful than Rupert in halting and rallying his men, most of whom also swept remorselessly on to Kineton.

As the Royalist infantry, led by Sir Jacob Astley, advanced, they would have had some inkling of the success enjoyed by the cavalry on each flank, and when the infantry of Colonel Charles Essex broke and ran before them, they must have thought the battle nearly won. But Sir John Meldrum's infantry brigade, supported by Colonel Thomas Ballard, held its ground, although greatly outnumbered. It was now that the initiative passed to the Parliamentarian cavalry, with Sir Philip Stapleton's and Sir William Balfour's cavalry charging out through the gaps in Meldrum's thinning ranks. The former was repulsed with heavy losses by Sir Nicholas Byron's brigade, but Balfour met with more success, breaking through Fielding's regiment and actually succeeding in getting in among the Royalists' cannon, which he proceeded to disable. In fact, Balfour's charge was so successful that he advanced to within striking distance of the king, who resolved to send the Prince of Wales and the Duke of York to safety. Narrowly avoiding capture, they made their way, under escort, to Arlescote House. Though this prize had slipped through his fingers, Balfour had done a great deal of damage and prudently withdrew.

The king's lifeguard, meanwhile, was locked in combat with Sir William Constable's regiment of foot. The honour of bearing the Royal Standard had been given to Sir Edmund Verney. He wore no armour and it is said that he had a premonition of his death. Struck down by Ensign Arthur Young, Verney's hand had to be hacked from his lifeless body, so tightly did it grasp the banner. The banner was actually in enemy hands for only six minutes, being rescued by a Captain Smith, who was knighted for his deed on the following day and who was to meet his own end two years later at Cheriton.

The victorious Royalist cavalry charges were halted with the arrival of Colonel John Hampden, whose brigade, ably assisted by one Captain Oliver Cromwell, checked the ardour of the more eager Cavaliers at what is now Prince Rupert's Headland. The confusion was frightful, many of the over-confident Royalist horsemen being cut down.

Supported by such cavalry as managed to return to the field, the hard-pressed Royalist foot rallied and held their ground. It was now growing dark and horse and foot of both armies had fought to a virtual standstill. In fact, both sides considered it wise to withdraw to their pre-battle positions and, although each claimed a victory, the result was clearly a draw. After a bitterly cold night, neither side felt sufficiently confident to renew hostilities. For three or four hours, each army kept a wary eye on the other. Essex was the first to lose his nerve, deciding to withdraw to Warwick Castle, leaving the field of battle with its spoils, including seven precious field guns, to the Royalists. In this sense, the Royalists were right in claiming at least a moral victory.

# The Aftermath

In fact, the guns taken by the Royalists were of heavy calibre and proved a valuable addition to their limited firepower. Muskets, pikes and some armour were also acquired, together with some standards and colours. At the time, balancing the books in terms of capture and loss of regimental colours took precedence over matters of men and arms. As the years wore on, however, the positions became reversed as the Royalists, in particular, began to appreciate more the bread and butter issues affecting the survival of their cause.

Reliable estimates of casualties at Edgehill have been lost in the propaganda war waged by both sides, Parliamentarian pamphleteers, for example, publicizing losses of three thousand Royalists against three hundred Roundheads. Most probably, casualties were light and evenly balanced, with a total of around fifteen hundred dead. Many more would have been seriously wounded and there were a great number of desertions, swelling the final 'casualty' figure into an unreal total.

A moral victory it may have been, but by failing to press on to London, Charles did not take full tactical advantage of his position, which, if capitalized upon, should have won him the war. Had he made haste for the capital, the element of surprise would have been his. Instead, he loitered in taking the relatively insignificant Banbury Castle, from where he marched to Oxford which became his headquarters for the next four years. Essex, albeit belatedly, was the first to reach London, where his army was quickly reinforced, the capital itself becoming an impregnable fortress. Charles may have claimed to have won his first battle, but the war was already lost.

A curious footnote to the conflict is provided by a pamphlet published three months after the event entitled 'A Great Wonder in Heaven Shewing The Late Apparitions and Prodigious Noyes of War and Battels, seen on Edgehill near Keinton in Warwickshire'. The writer describes how, shortly after midnight on Christmas Saturday, some shepherds had heard 'the sound of drums afar off, and the noise of soldiers, as it were giving out their last groans'. The unwilling witnesses of these phenomena were then treated to a spectral re-enactment of the battle. On the next night, a similar experience befell 'more substantial' local inhabitants, notably a Justice of the Peace and the Minister, who attested to the 'adverse armies, fighting with as much spite and spleen as formerly'.

The king, then at Oxford, was informed of the proceedings and was so moved that he sent a party of officers and gentlemen to investigate. They, too, saw the apparitions and were able to recognize many of the ghostly participants, including Sir Edmund Verney, who had been killed, and Prince Rupert, who was still very much alive.

A search of the battlefield led to the discovery of some bodies, as yet unburied. As soon as these remains had been decently interred, the hauntings, apparently, ceased. Notwithstanding this exorcism, sightings of the ghosts of Edgehill have been reported down to the present day, most notably at midnight on 23 October.

This tale has many parallels throughout history – in fact, a similar ghostly replay at Naseby was recorded many years after the battle. Such stories may be attributable to mass hallucination, caused by food poisoning operating against a background of superstition. The 'poison' probably originated from grain infected by ergot fungus. If concentrated in bread, then the fungus can cause madness and, in extreme cases, death. Less harmful poisoning used to occur in the consumption of locally-produced ale. In these cases, the watered-down effects would involve mild hallucination. In seventeenth-century England men, women and children often consumed vast quantities of ale. It is also likely that the king's investigators partook of the Kineton brew, which worked upon them in the same way that it had worked upon the local populace.

# The Walk

**Distance:**   10½ miles (17 km)

Begin at Kineton. Going out of the village on Banbury Road, note the Carpenter's Arms to the left and the post office on the right. Further along on the right is a lay-by beside allotments, which usually affords some parking (point A). Continue on foot on the B4086. Out of Kineton, on the right-hand side of the road, is a small monument (Pathfinder 998 356504) (point B) commemorating the battle and standing on the spot occupied by Ramsay's Parliamentarian horse before they were swept from the field by Rupert's cavalry charge. The monument was erected at a later date – 1949. The inscription reminds one that at a point three-quarters of a mile to the south lies the supposed burial ground of many of the casualties. All the land to the left and right is bordered by Ministry of Defence 'Keep Out' warnings, which should be heeded. A single-track railway supply line crosses the main road twice before one reaches a road on the right leading to Radway.

Turn and follow this road. Valley Farm is on the left and the buildings at the far end of the second field past the farm may be taken to roughly mark the site of 'King's Leys Barn', where tradition has it, Charles spent the night after the battle. Walk down into Radway and at the green, keep to the left. Turn left at the junction and on the right, there is a footpath. Take this path

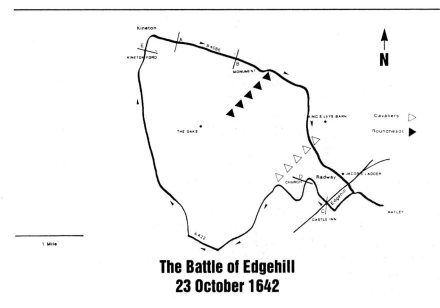

## The Battle of Edgehill
## 23 October 1642

and follow it through the gate and over the stile to emerge into a broad expanse of pasture. The path lies straight ahead. The climb is a gradual one and quite manageable. Nearing the top, aim for the stone seat ahead. After getting one's breath back, follow the path into Castle Wood. At the other side of a small clearing is a flight of stone steps, known as Jacob's Ladder. Walk to the top and continue on to Edgehill, emerging on to the main road.

Turn to the left and take the road to Ratley, almost diagonally opposite. Walk into Ratley, going down the hill into the village (down the High Street, past the post-box). The High Street develops into Church Street, with St Peter's church on the right (Pathfinder 1021 383473). Enter the church, which is open to visitors, to collect one of the useful 'Ratley and District Brief Historical Notes' booklets. Leaving the church, retrace your steps. Up to the left, an old castle mound is clearly discernible. Just beyond the post-box, take the left turning and walk along this road. On the right-hand side (just past a concrete turning for farm vehicles) is a narrow public footpath. Follow this path back into Edgehill, emerging by the post office. Across the road is the Castle Inn (point C), where refreshment is available, probably by this stage more than welcome.

Emerging from the inn, take the footpath down through the wood (running by the side of the inn). This leads back into Radway and resembles very closely the path leading up the hill – even to a stone bench at the foot of the wooded path. (In fact, this would have been a much steeper climb.) Emerging from the woods, pause to take in the panoramic view. Straight ahead are the stone bunkers of the Ordnance Depot, the area where the Roundheads would have been deployed. The Royalists would have been

The view from Castle Inn. The Cavalier centre and right wing were deployed to the left of the picture, facing the Roundhead centre and left wing in the middle distance.

gathered on the plain, beyond Radway church (look for the tower in the right foreground).

Walk straight down into Radway, hugging the field boundary to the right. A gate leads through from the field to a farm track, which develops into a metalled road, passing the very picturesque Radway Grange (Pathfinder 1021 368481). At the T-junction, turn to the left and follow the road around to St Peter's (point D). Enter the church to view the Kingsmill Monument, a stone effigy of Henry Kingsmill, a Royalist infantry captain killed at Edgehill by a 'cannon bullet'. Emerging from the church, turn to the right and follow the road round to the right at the next junction. (The track off to the left is King John's Lane, the old Kineton to Radway road, which probably existed at the time of the battle.) Making a turn to the right, one will see King's Clump standing back from the road on the right-hand side, from which vantage point the king evaded capture while watching the battle. Follow this road, which makes another sharp turn, this time to the left. (The muddy track which continues straight on is a continuation of King John's Lane and, but for the Ministry of Defence restrictions, would lead walkers into the heart of the battlefield.)

The road runs past Westcote Farm, which occupies what would have been the starting point of Wilmot's cavalry. This stretch of road provides a splendid view of the Edgehill escarpment. The Royalist army must have presented a magnificent sight, the regiments of foot in their bright red, white and blue coats and the cavalry officers in shining armour, or else handsomely attired in gold and silver lace.

Nearing the end of the road, opposite a large barn, cut across the pasture to join the A422 (now in sight). Using the wide grass verge, continue to the Kineton turn-off on the right. Follow this road for 3 miles into Little Kineton (Pathfinder 998 333504). As one approaches the track on the right, leading to Kent's Farm, look up to the right to view the main battlefield area. (A point to bear in mind is that almost the entire area – including the Edgehill escarpment – was unwooded, the clump of trees known as The Oaks being the position of Fielding's Royalist cavalry.)

Walking into Little Kineton, bear to the right and at the T-junction, take the right-hand fork to Kineton. Entering Kineton, the road dips sharply, marking Kineton Ford (point E), where many of the Parliamentarian horse were cut down. Take the first road on the right. At the top, turn right again, on to Banbury Road, and so back to the starting point in the lay-by by the allotments.

# Further Explorations

A useful departure point for a walk is the Edgehill Battle Museum, situated at Farnborough Hall (Landranger 151 4349), a shade too distant to be incorporated comfortably into the battlefield walk. The museum comprises an excellent on-going development of dioramas, displays and useful literature. Opening is seasonal on Wednesday and Saturday afternoons from April to September (tel: (0926) 332213 (office hours)).

The range of local exploration can be extended to include Upton House (Landranger 151 3645), a fine mansion built in the reign of William and Mary and boasting extensive and impressive gardens. The house, given to the National Trust by the Second Viscount Bearsted, contains an outstanding collection of works of art, from tapestries and porcelain to furniture and pictures (tel: (0295) 87266 for opening hours).

Sun Rising (Landranger 151 3645), on the brow of Edgehill, is contemporary with the battle and was, for many years, a coaching inn.

Of interest to the hardiest of railway ramblers will be the neglected route of the Stratford-upon-Avon and Midland Junction Railway at Kineton (Pathfinder 998 331512). This particular stretch of track was completed in 1871 and, in its heydey, Kineton was a busy station with many wealthy people who lived in the area travelling to London on a regular basis – including Lord Willoughby de Broke, 19th Baron, who was a director of the

SMJ. It is a portion of this railway that runs across the B4086 into the Central Ammunition Depot.

Also of interest are the remains of the Edgehill Airfield (Landranger 151 3642), now used as the base for a gliding club. Completed in October 1941 as a relief facility for Moreton-in-the-Marsh, Edgehill initially accommodated Wellingtons which took part in the raids on Essen and Cologne. Subsequently, its open position, with unobstructed approaches, led to it being chosen as a testing site for prototype jet-engined aircraft. Because the ground falls away sharply to the west, the airfield control tower was of an unusual two-storey design, providing the additional height needed for an effective watch to be maintained. The remains of the tower, together with examples of other typical wartime airfield architecture can still be seen. The airfield is well worth a visit.

If, as advised, the battlefield is approached via the A41 and B4086, shortly before arriving at Edgehill, one would pass, on the left, Nadbury Camp (Landranger 151 3948), a large hill fort, one of a small line of forts running along the brow of the Edgehills, attesting to the area's military importance in prehistoric times.

The area is one of the few in which the Landranger map is probably of more relevance than the Pathfinder. This is partly because the battlefield area itself is a large one and a smaller scale is useful for an 'at a glance' appraisal. The battlefield area stands out as being particularly devoid of public footpaths, but this should not be allowed to detract from the richness of walking opportunities in general. Immediately behind the Edgehills, to the south-east, are a selection of Oxfordshire circular walks, providing some of the most rewarding rambling to be found anywhere in the country.

## Further Information

Kineton lies in the middle of a triangle formed by the old Fosse Way, the A422 Stratford-upon-Avon to Banbury road and A41 Warwick to Banbury road. It is best approached by the latter road, and then the B4086 running up Edgehill and on to Kineton, which provides some stunning views. Long-distance travellers may prefer to use the M40, leaving at junction 12 and taking the B4451 directly into Kineton.

The closest railway station is Banbury (telephone (0295) 262256 for details of services). If you are travelling by coach, telephone 021 622 4373 for National Express services.

Relevant Ordnance Survey maps are Landranger 151 and Pathfinder 1021. Definitive reading is still provided by Peter Young's *Edgehill 1642: The Campaign and The Battle* (Roundwood Press, 1967).

# 9
# THE BATTLE OF CHALGROVE FIELD
## 18 June 1643

## *The Road to Chalgrove Field*

The year 1643 began with Sir Ralph Hopton and Sir Bevil Grenville, grandson of Sir Richard Grenville, capturing a Parliamentary fleet that had been blown off course into Falmouth. The booty taken then helped in the raising of an army which defeated a Parliamentarian army, led by the Earl of Stamford, at Braddock Down, on 19 January. By the end of February, Lichfield, Tamworth, Stafford and Ashby de la Zouch were all in Royalist hands. Early in March, Lichfield was temporarily lost, but even here, fortune favoured the king, because the Parliamentarian commander, Lord Brooke, was killed. (Brooke was the likely successor to Essex as Commander-in-Chief.) At Hopton Heath, later the same month, the Parliamentarians suffered a further defeat that paved the way for the reoccupation of Lichfield in April. On 16 May, at Stratton, near Bude, Stamford was again trounced by Hopton. Outnumbered by more than two to one and with Stamford occupying an almost impregnable hill-top position, Hopton still contrived to put the Parliamentarians to flight. In the north, too, encouraging progress was being made. Sir Hugh Cholmley, the governor of Scarborough, transferred his allegiance to Charles, and with him came Scarborough Castle. An impressive structure on a formidable site, the castle was never taken by force, remaining the sole Royalist port on the east coast throughout the war. In the West Riding, on 30 March, Lord Goring attacked and bested Sir Thomas Fairfax at Seacroft Moor. Everywhere, it seemed, the Royalist cause was gaining the upper hand.

Despite all the Royalist success, however, Charles remained vulnerable. Although victories were celebrated in the south-west and in the north, Oxford, the king's capital, was a scant 60 miles from London. One keen Parliamentary thrust at this, the Royalist heart, could end the war. Supplying the town with food and ammunition proved a constant headache.

The colleges were turned into arsenals and granaries and the college plate was melted down to make coinage. The few scholars who stuck it out were eventually used as forced labour in construction of the siegeworks.

In mid-April 1643, Essex, commanding an army of nearly twenty thousand men, laid siege to Reading, a mere 30 miles from Oxford. Not surprisingly, Charles viewed the lifting of the siege as top priority and Rupert, then in the process of recapturing Lichfield, was ordered to join his sovereign in a combined relief expedition. By 26 April, uncle and nephew were outside Reading, at Caversham, attempting to soften up Parliamentary resistance with an artillery barrage. The Royalist governor, Sir Arthur Aston, had been injured and Colonel Richard Fielding had taken over. By the time Charles had engaged Essex, Fielding had already begun negotiations for the surrender of the town and he felt honour-bound not to go back on them. So, Reading was lost. True to form, the king felt that Fielding should be put to death, and the wretched man was saved only by Rupert's personal intervention.

Following his success at Reading, Essex felt sufficiently confident to manoeuvre closer to Oxford. Basing himself at Thame, he was now only 10 miles distant. From Thame, he began to edge closer and closer towards his goal, first Wheatley and then Islip being probed for weaknesses. The troops were quartered both in Thame and in surrounding villages, and communication between the various camps was inefficient. Such a situation could be exploited by an enterprising opponent – which is exactly what happened.

## The Battle of Chalgrove Field

While quartered at Oxford, Rupert was approached by a Colonel Urry, a professional turncoat, of the type more usually associated with the Wars of the Roses than the Civil War. The artful Urry brought the tempting intelligence that the Parliamentary paymaster, in charge of a sum in excess of £20,000, was en route to Thame to pay the Roundhead troops. Rupert's response was characteristically bold. Giving but little consideration to the possibility that Urry might be a Parliamentarian spy, the Prince resolved to intercept and appropriate the wage packets.

On 17 June, Rupert left the Royalist capital, accompanied by eighteen hundred men. Early the following morning, he reached Postcombe, a hamlet near Chinnor, where he trounced the Parliamentarian guard. Immediately pushing on to Chinnor itself, the Royalists again surprised the Parliamentarian garrison, killing and capturing nearly two hundred dragoons. The exercise, although a splendid example of cut and thrust guerilla warfare, failed in its objective, for the paymaster's convoy – then in the locality – in response to the alarums and excursions, took refuge in the woods.

Having failed in his mission, and in the knowledge that the Roundheads were now fully aware of his position, Rupert had to engineer a withdrawal to Oxford. The route via Thame would be barred, and so he swept south to Chislehampton. His progress was slow – his force had been on the move since the previous afternoon and had seen action twice – and by mid-morning, skirmishes with Roundhead advance guards were already taking place.

At about nine o'clock, Rupert halted in a field near the village of Chalgrove, 3 miles from the Chislehampton crossing. Dragoons and foot were sent on to secure the bridge, while the cavalry regiment remained drawn up under cover of a hedge. Although the Prince's aides advised him to hasten the retreat, he was able to see that disaster could easily result if his men were caught crossing the river. On the other side of the hedge there appeared his Roundhead pursuers, under the command of Sir Philip Stapleton. The size of Stapleton's force was given as three hundred by Essex (in whose interest it was to minimize), while according to Cavalier estimates, the number was nearer eight hundred. Perhaps five hundred would be nearer the mark, but certainly the Roundheads were heavily outnumbered and it would have suited them to continue harrying Rupert at a safe distance until reinforcements appeared.

Then, in true Cavalier fashion, Rupert spurred on his horse and leapt the hedge, followed by the lifeguard. As usual, the Prince seemed to possess a charmed life and, although the Roundhead dragoons picked off several of the Royalists while this manoeuvre was taking place, Rupert himself remained unscathed. Rupert's regiment of horse, in more conventional fashion, rode round the hedge. The dragoons facing Rupert fled but, to its credit, the remaining Roundhead horse tried to make a fight of it. In what was essentially a cavalry action, and being so heavily outnumbered, they stood little chance. The Royalists were able to outflank and, in only a short time, surround them. The Roundheads lost forty-five men and over one hundred were taken prisoner. The reserves of strength conjured up by the Royalists, who were weary even before the fight commenced, are to be much admired. Immediately afterwards, they pressed on to Chislehampton, where they crossed the river in safety, reaching Oxford by two o'clock in the afternoon.

## *The Aftermath*

The Royalists attached great – but unwarranted – importance to Chalgrove Field, which, after all, had been little more than a skirmish. The escapade itself confirmed Prince Rupert's daring. It was encounters such as this

John Hampden's death at Chalgrove Field was a great blow to the Parliamentarian cause. Hampden's refusal to pay 'Ship Money' had led to the rift between king and Parliament (National Portrait Gallery)

which established his reputation, even though the most colourful descriptions of his antics usually originated from his closest friends.

The most serious immediate consequence of the battle for the Roundheads was the death of one of the elder statesmen of the Parliamentary cause, John Hampden, whose refusal to pay ship money had precipitated the crisis which led to the Civil War. He had also been one of the five MPs whom the king had attempted to arrest in January 1642. Although his military career had been undistinguished, his bravery was beyond doubt. Having risen from his bed on hearing the general alarm, he had attached himself to Stapleton's command. In the thick of the fighting, he received two gunshot wounds in the shoulder, which occasioned him to desert the field before the conflict was over. A week later, despite the king's gallant offer to send his personal physician to attend upon him, he died.

Colonel Urry received a knighthood for his services and Rupert was able to march into Oxford with his prisoners and a selection of pennants and colours. As a result of the battle and, in particular, Hampden's death, it was claimed that the Parliamentarians suffered a serious loss of confidence, Essex returned to London, Parliamentarian leaders began bickering and the New Model Army was proposed. There is some element of truth in these exaggerated claims, but the cock-a-hoop Royalist attitude after success in a very minor engagement demonstrates their not inconsiderable relief in finding an occasion to celebrate.

In fact, although Essex did not lose his command until the end of 1644, he was compelled to abandon his Oxford campaign while, in London, there was some disquiet at the ease with which Rupert had marched through an area dominated by the Parliamentarian army. Although the paymaster's train had slipped through his fingers, Rupert was so encouraged that he was keen to make further sallies into Chiltern territory.

Bickering was a constant theme among commanders of both sides – as it is in all wars – and Chalgrove Field simply added fuel to a continuous process. As for the creation of the New Model Army – serious discussions did not begin until after February 1645.

The king may well have been better advised to concentrate his efforts upon the centre ground, yet as time wore on, he was to become more and more obsessed with the West Country. Less than two months after Chalgrove Field, he was to be found laying siege to Gloucester. Essex marched out from London at the head of an army some fifteen-thousand strong, and Charles was compelled to give way. On his return to London, Essex found his way blocked by the king, who had outmanoeuvred him. The two armies met at Newbury on 20 September 1643. The Royalist cavalry, accustomed to sweeping all before it, was severely mauled and, at the end of the day, it was Charles who had to withdraw, leaving Essex free to continue on his way.

Small, impromptu engagements, such as Chalgrove Field, where mobility was the key, were very much to Rupert's taste, whereas his style was totally unsuited to major, set-piece battles, in which disciplined infantry played an increasingly significant role.

# *The Walk*

**Distance:**   5½ miles (9 km)

Begin in Chalgrove (Pathfinder 1137 637969). Just off the High Street, adjacent to The Crown public house, there is a free public car-park, clearly marked. From the car-park (point A), turn right into the High Street, which eventually becomes Hampden Road. Walk on to the B480, Watlington to Stadhampton road. Cross over with care and keep on straight ahead.

The Hampden Monument (Pathfinder 1137 646972) quickly looms up on the right. At the time of writing (March 1993), plans are afoot to supplement the monument with a memorial plaque to Hampden and the

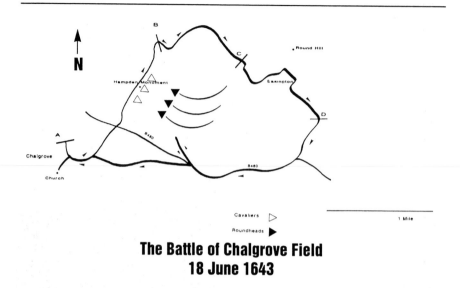

Cavaliers ▷

Roundheads ▶

1 Mile

# The Battle of Chalgrove Field
## 18 June 1643

battle at the other side of the road. Not many Chalgrove residents are aware of this, although some concern was expressed at the proposed visit of the 'Sealed Knot' to re-enact the battle in celebration of its three hundred and fiftieth anniversary. Comments are also made as to the stone monument's ugliness. In 1843, when the monument was erected, it probably did not appear quite so forbidding as it does today, standing as it does in a landscape dominated by the Chalgrove Airfield, on the left, and a developing industrial estate.

Continue until reaching an industrial estate entrance to the right bearing a public bridle-way sign (point B). Turn off, following the road around to the left and hugging the side of the building on the left. This leads into a field – look for the blue arrow bridle-way marker. The bridle-way comprises rather a muddy gap between hedge and planted field. At a metal gate on the left, there is another blue arrow marker pointing over the field to the right. Turn sharp right accordingly, aiming for a gate set in a copse directly opposite. The bridle-way across the field may not be visible, but set off in a straight line towards the gate.

When the course of a bridle-way is not readily apparent, one can often recognize the path by the tracks left by horse-riders. Thus, while horses often churn up a path, they can be of immeasurable assistance in keeping walkers on the 'straight and narrow' – especially when the bridle-way signs peter out, as they do now. Behind the gate is a path bordered with trees. Walk through here, and at the other side, a farm track may be seen in the middle distance, winding away up an incline towards the hamlet of Easington.

Hampden's Monument

At the farm track (point C), the bridle-way veers to the right, skirting the perimeter of the copse ahead. One cannot take this path because a home-made electrified fence bars the way. Therefore, follow the track itself to the farmyard. A sharp right-hand turn beyond the farmyard runs up into Easington (Pathfinder 1137 662971). Follow the narrow road up through the hamlet.

Shortly after leaving the hamlet, the road begins to run downhill, where it terminates in a T-junction with another minor road (point D). A right turn on to this road leads back towards Chalgrove. Eventually, the minor road joins up with the B480 and here, for a while, progress is a little tricky. The road is a busy one and the grass verge is not walkable, so be ready to step off the road in the face of oncoming traffic. A little further on, the verge does become walkable and, as Chalgrove comes into view, it broadens out to provide more comfortable walking.

When Chalgrove is well in sight, look for an unmarked road off to the right. This road leads to Hampden's Monument. Walk a little way along this road, where 'Chalgrove Field' can be seen to the right.

Now return to the main road. Opposite, is a public footpath sign leading to Chalgrove. It is well-trodden and easy to follow. If ploughing does render it difficult to recognize half-way through, it helps to know that it runs straight. In good light, one can make out a small white sign in front of an area of newly-planted trees. Reaching this sign, one can see that it has been erected by the Country Landowners Association, and assures one that landowners welcome caring walkers. The path leads out into a field once more before one takes sharp right turn along a comfortable grassy path into Chalgrove. Emerging from the path, aim at the white cottage in the High Street.

Turn left into the High Street and proceed to Church Lane. To look at St Mary's church, turn down Church Lane and follow the road. The church, which is open to the public, is well worth a visit and contains remarkable and lovingly-restored medieval murals. Leaving the church, turn left and re-enter the High Street a little further along. By this time, refreshment at The Crown bordering the car-park may well be in order. Directly opposite is the Red Lion, a curious arrangement for such a small town. The latter establishment is actually church property.

Geographically, as far as the Midlands is concerned, Chalgrove occupies a peripheral position. However, as the action, in part, was intended to divert Parliamentarian attention from Oxford, it is felt that the battle has enough of a 'south Midlands' flavour to warrant inclusion in the present volume.

# Further Explorations

Oddly enough, considering its Civil War pedigree, Oxfordshire is not over-endowed with sites worthy of further exploration. The administration of the royal capital itself was organized around the colleges, which lost not only their plate but also their students and buildings.

A village with an illustrious Civil War connection is Woodstock (Landranger 164 4416). The king visited Woodstock Manor for hunting and the house was damaged when under siege in the spring of 1646. Eventually, it was demolished in the eighteenth century and its memory has now been all but erased by the magnificent Blenheim Palace. In 1649, Parliamentary commissioners arrived at Woodstock to organize the destruction of the park and the confiscation of its furniture. During their stay, the commissioners' work was subjected to disruption by evil spirits. Furniture and pewter ware were thrown around, candles were extinguished and one of the party was doused with ditch water as he slept – all by an invisible and malevolent agency – while the hours of darkness were punctuated by unearthly cries and roars. At the end of three weeks, the commissioners fled. Many years later, the Clerk to the Commissioners, Joseph Collins, announced that he had been responsible for the haunting. A confirmed Royalist and practical joker, he was acquainted with a network of secret passages in the house and, with the assistance of the servants, had been able to orchestrate the reign of terror.

Faringdon (Landranger 163 2895), a Royalist outpost and scene of sundry hostilities, was attacked by the Roundheads in 1645. The Pye family of Faringdon House was one of many families rent asunder by the conflict. So it came to pass that Sir Robert Pye, who had chosen the Parliamentary cause, laid siege to his own home. Sir Robert has since been identified as the headless ghost that haunts Faringdon's All Saints' church.

John Hampden's ghost is said to haunt his local tavern, The Plough in Clifton Hampden (Landranger 164 5495), while The George in Wallingford (Landranger 175 8960) is reputedly haunted by the ghost of a mistress of the king, who pined away when she learned of his execution.

At Burford (Landranger 163 2412), in 1649, mutineers from the New Model Army were captured and incarcerated in St John the Baptist's church, the font still bearing graffiti as evidence of the occurrence. The church should be open and is worth a visit.

Abingdon (Landranger 164 4997) has a chequered history for the Civil War period. Its proximity to Oxford endowed it with a certain significance and the king often held important meetings there. Towards the end of May 1643, the Royalist garrison was abandoned in a drive for troops to defend the royal capital and although attempts were made to regain it, the town remained in Parliamentarian hands for the rest of the war. With only 6 miles between Abingdon and Oxford, this must have been a source of continuous Royalist concern. Rupert's failure to occupy the town in January 1645 was one of only two – the other, his unsuccessful defence of Bristol, later in the year, signalling the end of the Royalist cause.

# *Further Information*

Chalgrove Field is quite accessible via the M40. The A329 from junction 7 will take one there. From the south, take the A34 to Didcot, to link up with the A329 via the A4130.

Oxford is well served by all public transport. For rail information, telephone (0865) 722333 and for National Express coaches (0865) 791579. For details of Oxford City Council bus services between Oxford and Chalgrove, telephone (0865) 711312.

Oxford Tourist Office (tel: (0865) 726871) has further details about the area and its facilities.

Relevant Ordnance Survey maps are Landrangers 163, 164 and 175, and

Pathfinder 1137. Opportunities for further reading are limited. Philip Warner's *British Battlefields: The Midlands* (Osprey, 1973) has a useful chapter. Howard Green's *Guide to the Battlefields of Britain and Ireland* (Constable, 1973) also includes a résumé of events and an account of the battle can also be found in *John Hampden the Patriot* by John Adair (1976).

# 10
# THE BATTLE OF WINCEBY
## 11 October 1643

## *The Road to Winceby*

Reading through standard military histories, one could be forgiven for thinking that the east of England has played very little part in hosting the battles which have shaped the course of history. In fact, over the centuries, the eastern counties have staged many engagements – and doubtless many more, long forgotten. Granted, some of those encounters would have been seemingly small skirmishes but a battle's significance cannot always be measured according to the number of participants and casualties, and lesser battles have sometimes been the catalyst for greater events. Mortimer's Cross, for example, was a relatively lightweight affair, but led directly to the crowning of a new king. Another such minor conflict occurred in the Lincolnshire hamlet of Winceby and was important because it heralded the 'arrival' of Oliver Cromwell.

The first half of 1643 had witnessed much action in the south-west, with battles at Braddock Down, Stratton, Lansdown Hill and Roundway Down. In the north, at the beginning of September, the Royalists, under the Marquess of Newcastle, laid siege to Hull – a state of affairs which Parliament did not intend to tolerate. In Norfolk, King's Lynn was also under siege, only here the positions were reversed: the Royalists were holding out against the Parliamentarians under the Earl of Manchester. Colonel Cromwell was among the besieging troops and Manchester, who had no great love for the man, was pleased to send him on an expedition through Lincolnshire to Hull. Accompanied by Lord Willoughby, whom he had collected at Boston, Cromwell managed to cross the River Humber and effect an entry into Hull. Not only was Cromwell able to get in, but Sir Thomas Fairfax, with twenty troops of horse, was able to leave with him.

King's Lynn fell on 16 September, enabling Manchester to link up with Cromwell and Fairfax, by advancing to Boston. This put the

Parliamentarians within striking distance of another Royalist garrison, at Bolingbroke Castle. Bolingbroke, built in the fourteenth century by John of Gaunt, was the birthplace of Henry IV, and so was destined to play a role in two civil wars, three hundred years apart.

The Royalists thus found themselves rapidly being overhauled in the east, their main difficulty being a shortage of manpower. This was to prove a problem throughout the war years. The usual solution was to pare down to a bare minimum the strength of garrisons not currently under threat. By creaming off troops from Newark, Lincoln and Gainsborough, a force of some two thousand five hundred was assembled in order to meet Manchester's advance. The action was justifiable, for if Manchester was allowed to proceed unhindered, both Lincoln and Gainsborough, which had only recently changed hands, could be threatened.

The Royalist task force was under the command of Sir William Widdrington, the Royalist Commander-in-Chief in Lincolnshire, and Sir John Henderson, the first governor of Newark. Manchester, meanwhile, lost no time in investing Bolingbroke. He also took the precaution of sending Fairfax to do some prospecting around Horncastle to the north. On 10 October, Fairfax encountered the Royalists. There was little his small body of horse could do to halt the advance, save to slow it down by skirmishing while conducting an orderly retreat towards Manchester's main force, which was, by that time, marching from Bolingbroke towards Horncastle on a route which would take it through Winceby. In fact, Manchester marched through the village, less than a mile beyond which he discovered the Royalists, perhaps marginally outnumbering him, drawing up in battle order.

## The Battle of Winceby

Manchester was keen on a confrontation, although in fairness, Cromwell was against it. Both armies occupied ridges about half a mile apart. In the middle was open ground, dipping slightly – not unlike the battlefield at Naseby. (Gentle slopes falling away from opposing vantage points constituted the preferred scenario for civil war battles.) Manchester organized a vanguard, comprising his own and Cromwell's regiments, supported by Fairfax in the rear. In front of both was a 'Forlorn Hope' of musketeers, commanded by Colonel Vermuyden. The foot, commanded by Sir Miles Hobart, had not yet arrived and Manchester hurried back to chase them up. The Royalist vanguard, composed of dragoons, was supported by three divisions of horse with Henderson on the left, Sir William Savile on the right and Widdrington in the rear. Neither Widdrington nor Manchester, it would appear, intended to lead from the front.

Battle commenced with the advance of the Royalist vanguard. Vermuyden responded, both sides dismounting and opening fire. Royalist and Parliamentary cavalry began down the slope from either ridge and Cromwell's horse was shot from beneath him. As he rose, he was knocked down by a redoubtable Cavalier, Sir Ingram Hopton. Had Hopton there and then dispatched the colonel, history, as they say, could have been changed. Probably acting from a sense of honour, he chose to take Cromwell prisoner, but in the confusion following the clash of the cavalry, Hopton, in paying more attention to his prospective prisoner than to his own safety, was killed. A Roundhead trooper provided Cromwell with a poor, replacement mount.

At this point, accounts of the battle become diversified. In view of Cromwell's subsequent reputation, it is, perhaps, understandable that some poetic licence should be applied in describing his role. According to the popular version, he remounted, rallied his troops and led a second charge which put the opposition to flight. This is unlikely as he would have needed time to acclimatize himself to his new horse, and while he was thus incapacitated, the action continued. There was a decisive Roundhead assault, but it was led by Fairfax, who moved up on to the ridge to the right

The victor of Winceby, Sir Thomas Fairfax, was the best of the Parliamentarian commanders and was selected to lead the New Model Army on its formation (City of York Leisure Services)

and attacked diagonally across the hollow. Instead of meeting Fairfax head-on, Savile's horsemen broke and fled and as was often the case, the collapse of one wing quickly led to a rout.

Despite the weariness of their mounts, the Roundheads pressed home their attack, Savile's men being driven back, off the road and into the fields. They were halted in their flight by a high hedge. The good news that the hedge was broken by a gate quickly turned into bad news as it was discovered that the gate opened inwards, towards the mass of horsemen converging on it. Unable to open it, the desperate Royalists were cut to pieces, the spot acquiring the graphic title Slash Hollow. The dismounted dragoons stood no chance at all and were slaughtered where they stood.

Henderson and Widdrington's line of retreat was more open, but they still fared badly, many Royalists falling to the east of Winceby in Snipe Dale, which, at the time, was marshland. The fighting itself had been short and sharp, and was over before the arrival of Manchester's infantry, which was sufficiently fresh to join in the pursuit for several miles. The surviving Royalists fell back to Lincoln, while the victorious Roundheads settled for a well-earned night's rest in Horncastle.

## *The Aftermath*

Arguments that the victory at Winceby raised the morale of the Roundhead cavalry are largely academic, and too much meaning should not be read into the trouncing of a saddle-weary force of garrison troops. Had Prince Rupert's lifeguards been present, the outcome could well have been very different – as it had been at Chalgrove Field earlier in the year (see p. 93). Doubtless, Fairfax knew this, yet he was tempted to embroider a tale or two of his own. As the battle drew to a close, he claimed to have heard artillery fire from Hull, which turned out to be his father, Lord Fairfax, making a sortie from the city, which led to Newcastle abandoning the siege. The fact that Hull was some 40 miles distant, means that the younger Fairfax must have been possessed of extraordinary powers of hearing. Widdrington wrote to Newcastle, apprising him of the situation and begging him to send reinforcements lest the whole county of Lincolnshire be lost. The Marquess, whose blockade of Hull had never been effective, obliged by raising the siege and setting out in the opposite direction, for York. It was in Widdrington's interest to over-react in fostering the impression of defeat at the hands of a particularly formidable opponent.

As for Cromwell, he had, in the first instance, advised against a fight. He had then suffered a fall, followed up by an assault by a Cavalier. Manchester made little effort to praise the colonel's part in the proceedings and, while acknowledging Fairfax's contribution, he stressed that the latter was merely carrying out his instructions. As it happened, no one was fooled and when the New Model Army was formed, Fairfax was placed in command.

Newcastle's siege of Hull would have collapsed regardless of the Winceby result. His troops comprised conscripts with no compunction about deserting the grand cause to return to their farms and trades. Cromwell had entered and left with comparative ease, and the besieged sallied forth from the city gates with such freedom that Newcastle must have wondered who was investing whom.

Even Bolingbroke Castle, which one might have expected to capitulate following Winceby, managed to hold out for another month. Lord Willoughby took over the siege begun by Manchester, but was unable to bring the garrison to its knees until 14 November. Six days later, on 20 November, Lincoln also fell to Parliament – only to change hands yet again in March of the following year.

Although neither Winceby, nor Cromwell's part in the victory, are deserving of too much praise, 1643 was, in the long term, to prove an important year. Cromwell's work in organizing the Eastern Association (an association of the East Anglian counties formed for the raising and training of troops) was tireless. From time to time, he would meet expenses out of his own pocket – a function which was not entirely a Royalist privilege – and lobbied continuously for emphasis to be placed on recruiting and training cavalry, as opposed to foot and musketeers. It was in Lincolnshire skirmishes, such as Winceby, that the Eastern Association forces gained invaluable experience. In due course, these troops, selected for both their religious zeal and their skills in the saddle, were used as a model for the development of the New Model Army, a body of trained and disciplined men, including in its ranks, Cromwell's own Ironsides, which was able to bring the conflict to a speedy conclusion in a matter of months, with victories at Marston Moor and Naseby.

# *The Walk*

**Distance:**   6 miles (10 km)

The starting point is the new country park development (Pathfinder 783 333680) (point A) in the woodland to the east of Winceby. The entrance is on the Horncastle to Spilsby low road, where car-parking and toilets are available.

Return to the road and turn to the right, a short distance along the verge

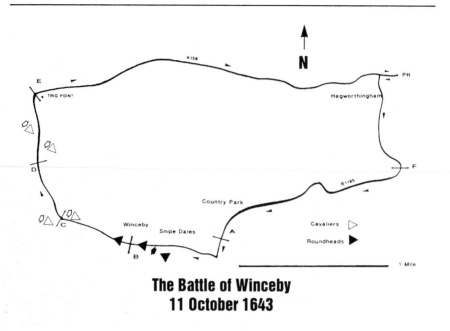

## The Battle of Winceby
## 11 October 1643

Winceby House comes into view, an imposing yellow-brick building in the Regency style (now a private farmhouse). To the right, adjoining the country park, is the Snipe Dales nature reserve – marshland in 1643 – where many of the Royalist dead lay. But this is anticipating events because the Roundheads are only now marching up from the Bolingbroke road to your left.

The Roundheads deployed on the crest of the hill, slightly beyond Winceby House (point B), and the occupants of the farm must have been busily engaged in putting up the shutters. The Royalists were further up the road, their advance positions equating with the Hameringham road and the reservoir on the near corner (point C) where the Royalist dragoons were drawn up. Now proceed along Slash Lane. Henderson came into view on the high ground to the right and Savile advanced from the left. Widdrington was still out of view in the rear.

Behind, following an exchange of gunfire, Cromwell's horse charged the Royalist dragoons. In the general mêlée which followed, Fairfax wheeled his cavalry around Cromwell's right, turning in front of Henderson to attack Savile. Savile's troops broke rank and fled across the field to the left – Slash Hollow. To the left there is a tract of woodland. Running through here is what used to be known as Winceby Beck, which trickled on as far as the road. Directly behind the beck was the hedge containing the gate on to which the fleeing Roundheads pressed – to be cut down by Fairfax's horse.

Walk a little way further up the road and where it bends to the right, the

Snipe Dale, the final resting place for many Royalists

grass verge on the left broadens out (point D). The present road is new. The old road to Horncastle followed straight on along what is now a bridle-path, and it is likely that the Roundheads' efforts to negotiate the gate in the hedge were aimed at gaining this road. Unfortunately, the bridle-path would appear to be in the process of being lost, and it seems likely that this ancient way, of historical significance, will be removed altogether.

Continue to the junction with the A158 (point E). Turning to the right, the corner can be cut by walking across a small grassy enclosure containing an Ordnance Survey trigonometrical pillar (Pathfinder 783 312696). Before the days of satellite technology, these trig points assisted map-makers by providing a firm base for theodolites in the measurement of angles and distances. Now, the Ordnance Survey has offered many of the redundant pillars for 'adoption' by groups and individuals interested in maintaining them. (See under Further Information.)

Keeping to the grass verge, walk along the A158, being especially vigilant for traffic on this busy road. The verge is wide and walking becomes increasingly easy as one progresses. The views over rolling fields both to left and right demonstrate why it is worth it. Past Highfield Farm (Pathfinder 783 326698), leave the main road. With care, cross over to the old road (which has been by-passed by a new stretch of A158) and continue in peace and tranquillity. This stretch of road can be followed all the way into

Hagworthingham. Ignore the 'No Through Road' sign and walk on, along the grass track, round to the right and so on to the concrete footpath leading into the village.

On the right is Church Lane, leading to Lusby, but don't turn straight-away. A little way further along the main road, on the left, is the George and Dragon, where refreshment may be taken before proceeding. Afterwards, walk down Church Lane, through the village, crossing the ford at the far end. Shortly after the ford, follow the footpath sign to the country park (point F). This is one of the new paths, the old path (still intact) running between two houses before the ford.

Follow the course of this path, bounded by barbed wire until, by hugging the field perimeters and turning sharply right, the country park development is reached. Walk around the perimeter of the pond and follow the wide grassy path. Keep straight on and don't stray from it. The grass path gives way to gravel and very soon, you will see a foot-bridge crossing a small waterfall to the left and, beyond it, a difficult-to-read sign indicating an 'easy' path to the car-park. In fact, this is a narrow, steep and winding path, although it does indeed lead into the car-park.

# Further Explorations

There are exciting opportunities for further exploration in the surrounding countryside of the Lincolnshire wolds. Just 4 miles distant is Horncastle, where a settlement was already established at the time of the Roman occupation. The Ninth Legion was active in the locality and, in AD 61, bore the brunt of Boadicea's revolt. Shortly afterwards, it disappeared from recorded history, constituting one of the greatest mysteries of all time. Remains of the 13 ft thick Roman wall can still be seen in the town in Bridge Street and in Wharf Road, where a portion of it has been incorporated into the public library.

As with many Mercian settlements, Horncastle suffered from the Danish invasions of the ninth century. In somewhat dubious commemoration of this event, the long-distance footpath, the Viking Way, passes through the town.

St Mary's church, dating from the twelfth century, is of interest because it contains a memorial to Sir Ingram Hopton, one of the casualties of Winceby, and also a brass dedicated to Sir Lionel Dymoke, the King's Champion.

To the south of Horncastle is Scrivelsby (Pathfinder 783 272661), home of the Dimmock family. Although Sir Thomas was beheaded before the Battle of Empingham (see p. 38), the Dimmocks continued to fill the King's Champion post until 1821, when the last ceremonial duties were performed for George IV. Although Scrivelsby Court no longer exists, the gateway to the estate, capped by a stone lion, has survived and is a curious sight in its isolation.

Continuing to move in an anti-clockwise direction from Horncastle, one arrives at East Kirkby (Pathfinder 783 333623), where the Lincolnshire Aviation Heritage Centre (telephone 07903 207 for details) is based on the former Second World War airfield. Opened in 1943, the airfield was constructed as a relief field for Scampton, Lancasters being based there until the end of the war. There is much to see both in terms of displays and airfield architecture. Perhaps the airfield ghost will also make an appearance.

An 'essential' visit is to Bolingbroke (accessible at any reasonable time), 2 miles to the north of East Kirkby and, in particular, to the castle (Pathfinder 783 349650), which does, after all, play a leading role in the approach to the action at Winceby. Following the Roundhead victory at Winceby, the Bolingbroke garrison was evacuated, the Royalists leaving behind some two hundred horses in the stables in their haste. At the time of the Civil War, the castle was still an imposing structure, probably having deteriorated very little since its great days two centuries before. After the siege, the castle was dismantled by the Roundheads and it subsequently declined into the pitiful ruin which stands today. The siege was also responsible for the destruction of Bolingbroke church which had to be rebuilt following the Restoration.

# Further Information

Winceby lies between Lincoln and Skegness – the destination for holiday-makers in the bygone days of the 'factory fortnight' August holiday. In the heart of rural Lincolnshire, Winceby is not easily accessible by road. The A15, Ermine Street, constitutes the main arterial approach on a north–south axis, with the A57 and the A46 converging on Lincoln from the north-west and south-west respectively. The A158 takes one from Lincoln and, once through Horncastle, look out for the A1115 Winceby road. The country park is signposted.

British Rail runs services to both Lincoln and Skegness. The Lincoln Inter-City service is good – businessmen have bought houses in Lincoln, commuting daily to London on the strength of it. For British Rail services in the area, telephone (0522) 539502. For National Express services, telephone (0733) 237141. Regular buses run via Hagworthingham. Up to a dozen companies appear to share the timetable, information concerning which can be obtained by telephoning (0522) 553135.

The relevant Ordnance Survey maps are Landranger 122 and Pathfinder 783. Further reading on the subject of the battle is not very prolific. One of the best accounts is to be found in A.H. Burne's *The Great Civil War 1642–46* (Methuen, 1959). Also see *The Battle of Winceby* by D. Frampton and P. Garnham (Partizan Press).

If interested in looking after one of the old trig points in your area, contact Ordnance Survey, Romsey Road, Maybush, Southampton SO9 4DH, or telephone (0703) 792635.

# 11
# THE BATTLE OF CROPREDY BRIDGE
## 29 June 1644

## *The Road to Cropredy Bridge*

The opening months of 1644 were not good for the Royalists. In March, at Cheriton Wood, near Winchester, the Roundheads, led by Sir William Waller, thrashed a Royalist army under the Earl of Forth and Lord Hopton. There were important territorial gains for Parliament and the overweening confidence of the Royalist cavalry was distinctly blunted. The most significant outcome for Parliament, however, was the consequent Royalist retreat from the West Country, which meant that Charles was in danger of being pinned down within an ever-decreasing circle radiating from Oxford. Unfortunately for Waller, some of his regiments decided that they had done their work in quite a satisfactory way and marched back to London, to their shops and businesses, so that he was unable to follow up his advantage.

While the king seemed to be continually diversifying his forces (and, in the process, weakening the fronts through which he might launch an attack on the enemy), it was the Parliamentary strategy to concentrate its armies. This was tactically sound – up to a point – decisions having to be made as to whether a recently-taken town should be adequately garrisoned or left wide open to attack. At this time, Parliament was unable to unite its armies as the Earl of Manchester was tied down at Lincoln, which he took on 6 May before marching up into Yorkshire for an encounter with Prince Rupert.

Without Rupert's guidance, the royal resolve tended to waver and Charles began to worry about the security of Oxford. By abandoning Reading, he was able to add two thousand five hundred troops to the Oxford garrison, but even with reinforcements, it seemed that the royal capital could not withstand a concerted Roundhead assault. Essex was marching up from London, while Waller advanced via Farnham, Basing and the newly-abandoned Reading. Had the two armies joined up, as planned, then Oxford might have been seriously threatened. However, it was not only the Royalist general staff which suffered from internal strife and discord. Essex was resentful of his colleagues, of Manchester and Waller in particular, and took every opportunity to both belittle their efforts and decry their capabilities as field commanders. Thus, cooperation between Essex and Waller was poor and the king was permitted a breathing space in which he was able to slip out of Oxford with his army and lead his adversaries on a wild goose chase through the Cotswolds.

Eventually, Essex gave up the chase and marched south-west to Lyme to relieve the siege of the town being conducted by Prince Maurice. Although unsupported, Waller continued the chase while Charles, now reinforced and at the head of about ten thousand men, began to look for an opportunity to take the offensive. It seemed certain that a battle would now take place. The questions were when and where would it happen?

By 26 June, much to his relief, Waller himself had received reinforcements from Warwick and Coventry and had reached Kineton. Now it was Parliament's turn to be alarmed. If Charles was able to inflict a decisive defeat upon Waller, London would be open to him. The following day, the king decided that Waller must be brought to battle without further delay and on 28 June, there was some preliminary skirmishing and jockeying for position in the vicinity of Banbury.

Sir William Waller, the Parliamentarian commander at Cropredy Bridge, was an able soldier who proposed the formation of the New Model Army (Goodwood Collection)

# The Battle of Cropredy Bridge

By three o'clock in the morning of 29 June the Roundhead army had occupied a commanding position to the south-west of Banbury, on Crouch Hill. In an effort to entice Waller away from this advantageous spot, Charles marched away towards Daventry. Waller took the bait but hedged his bets by choosing to shadow the Royalists via the Southam road. This must have been a sight to behold: both armies marching almost parallel, a distance of a mile apart and separated only by the River Cherwell. As the roads approach Cropredy, they diverge somewhat and Waller, anxious to maintain his parallel course with the Royalists, took the Great Bourton road, leading to Cropredy Bridge, the strategic importance of which the Royalists were quick to appreciate, dispatching a party of dragoons to hold it until the army had passed by.

At this juncture, Royalist scouts reported three hundred Roundhead cavalry some 2 miles ahead, apparently trying to link up with Waller. In their efforts to intercept this body of horse, the Royalist column became invitingly strung-out, and Waller conceived and implemented a bold plan. One detachment of horse, under Lieutenant-General John Middleton, was sent on to Cropredy Bridge, while another, led by Waller himself, crossed the river at Slat Mill, 1 mile to the south. (By this time it was about one o'clock in the afternoon.) The aim was to slice the Royalist column in two and trap the rear half in a pincer movement. In theory, it was a brilliant tactical manoeuvre. In practice, it all went horribly wrong. The Earl of Cleveland, at the head of the Royalist rearguard, deployed his men to meet Middleton's onslaught, while the Earl of Northampton, bringing up the rear, repelled Waller's advance from Slat Mill. Some credit is also due to Sir Bernard Astley's infantry supporting both Northampton and Cleveland.

In fact, the Roundhead plan did meet with limited success, leading to a pursuit of the scattered Royalist horse and foot as far as Hay's Bridge, about three-quarters of a mile to the north – but, even here, the assault foundered with the Royalists staging a determined rearguard action. By this time, of course, Charles was aware of the situation and promptly sent troops, commanded by Lord Bernard Stuart, back over Hay's Bridge, which he had crossed while his rearguard lingered all of 2 miles behind.

Regrouping, Middleton launched a second assault. This time, he was beaten back to the bridge by Cleveland who, with Stuart's timely assistance, captured the bulk of the Parliamentarian guns. Waller drew back across the river to a position on high ground near Bourton, leaving detachments to hold Cropredy Bridge and the ford at Slat Mill. Charles, meanwhile, drew

Cropredy Bridge

up his forces on the Daventry road at Williamscot. Thus both armies once again faced each other, divided only by the River Cherwell.

Charles determined to press home his advantage and ordered assaults on both the bridge and the mill. The ford was quickly overrun, but the Roundheads at the bridge held out. As the day wore on, both sides contented themselves by firing ineffectual artillery broadsides. The day certainly belonged to Charles, and either through inherent vacillation or magnanimity, he sent a message to Waller, offering an amnesty to all in the Parliamentary army who would lay down their arms – terms with which Waller said he had no authority to comply.

## The Aftermath

Cropredy Bridge amounted to little more than a side-show, the major theatre of war at this stage in the conflict being the north of England. The most immediate significant result of the Royalist victory was that it guaranteed Oxford's security – for the time being at least. Casualties were light. Underestimated by Royalist sympathizers as between 14 and 20,

Royalist dead must have numbered at least 50. Roundhead casualties were certainly much higher – most likely in the region of two hundred. Although hostilities continued for most of the day, the main armies assumed a stand-off position, such fighting as there was being fragmented into several contributory actions. The number of prisoners taken by both sides was also low, probably in the ratio of 4 to 1 in favour of the Royalists.

Whether it is described more fairly as a battle or a skirmish, Cropredy Bridge has occasionally been cited by military historians as an example of Charles's competent generalship, yet it is difficult to see how such an argument can be sustained. As Prince Rupert observed, the Royalist column should never have been permitted to become so thinly strung-out in the first instance, while Waller's master plan was thwarted largely by Cleveland's initiative in turning to meet Middleton's charge. It had not been the king's intention to engage Waller at that particular time. Charles's contribution to the victory consisted of his decision to dispatch troops from the vanguard to support Cleveland's action.

On the other hand, the king does appear to have been arriving at considered decisions throughout. This may have resulted from Rupert's absence because, more often than not, Charles found himself having to referee in the constant bickering between his nephew and the royal advisers – including Digby, Percy, and Goring – a problem with which, in this instance, he did not have to contend. The decision-making process was therefore rendered considerably more straightforward. And important strategic decisions did have to be made, with the intelligence that another Parliamentarian army, under Major-General Richard Browne, lay at Buckingham and, in all probability, would be marching to join Waller. In view of his own need for fresh troops and provisions, Charles decided not to linger, but to abandon Waller to his Bourton Hill stronghold.

It had been Charles's original plan to march south but, afraid of being caught between Waller and Browne, this was severely modified into a decision to cross the Cherwell and strike west. Charles reached Evesham on 3 July and it was here that he received news of Rupert's defeat at Marston Moor – a battle which tended to place the Cropredy Bridge affair in some perspective.

Following their trouncing, the spirits of Waller's troops were at an understandably low ebb. Waller and Browne were scheduled to link up at Towcester, where both commanders experienced problems with their rank and file – London and Home Counties men impatient to be off to their homes once more. Waller advised his Parliamentary masters of his intention to follow the king, assurances which carried little conviction due to the sorry condition of his army. All pretence of following the Royalist spoor was abandoned when, with the news of the Marston Moor triumph, hundreds of

London troops deserted. They thought the war was surely now all but won. Eventually, Waller returned to London, abandoning the remains of his army at Abingdon.

## *The Walk*

**Distance:**  3½ miles (5½ km)

The best way to approach Cropredy is via the A361 Banbury to Daventry road. Take the Williamscot to Cropredy turn-off and, approaching Cropredy, the Bridge Stores is on your right. The shop sells a variety of groceries, as well as maps, postcards and a small booklet on the history of the village. Parking is available in a lay-by opposite. This is the starting point (Pathfinder 1022 469466) (point A).

Ahead is one of the two village bridges which cross the Oxford Canal. Walk down to the canal tow-path, turning to the left (towards Banbury) at the bottom. The canal runs from Oxford to Coventry and was used to carry coal from the industrial Midlands down to Banbury, Oxford and the Thames. Today, many people actually live on the barges on the canal, as

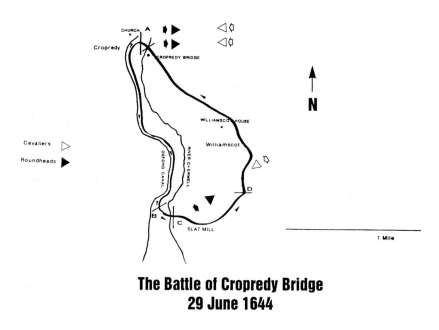

**The Battle of Cropredy Bridge
29 June 1644**

well as spending time at the weekends relaxing on it. Canal walks are becoming increasingly popular although, like railway walks, circular rambles are not always easy to organize. Close to Cropredy are the permanent moorings, which means that the path is well trodden. Maintenance is a problem, although where the path was once dangerously narrow in parts, it has now been shored up and widened.

As one clears the village, the going becomes easier. To the right, coming into view, is Bourton House, behind which stands the village of Great Bourton, on high land which enabled Waller to see the Royalist army moving along the Cherwell Valley to the left. A little further along, to the left, Williamscot House can be seen. Opposite Williamscot, walk under a brick bridge, continuing along until farm buildings loom up on your right – the site of another bridge, which is the point at which one leaves the tow-path (Pathfinder 1022 472451) (point B).

Scrambling up the embankment on the left – where others have gone before – one can squeeze through into the fields. Looking ahead slightly to the right, look for a foot-bridge which crosses the Cherwell. Walking down to this foot-bridge, look to the left and to see the remains of Slat Mill. One of the advantages of walking out of season is that undergrowth does not obscure features of interest. Sadly, these ruins are gradually being whittled away, but it was at this point that Waller crossed the river – at that time, a much more vigorous affair than it is today.

The remains of Slat Mill, where Waller effected a crossing of the River Cherwell

Cross the river by the foot-bridge (point C) and aim for the middle of the hedgerow at the far end of the field ahead (there is an old farm building to the right). This part of the walk is a bridle-path, so horseshoe tracks should help you keep to the path. Cross over into the next field and once more aim for the gate at the centre of the hedgerow at the far end. The road is now quite close to the right, where Waller's cavalry veered off to take up the pursuit on Williamscot Hill.

Entering the third field, begin a steep climb, hugging the remains of the hedgerow. At the top, look down to the left, picking out some farm buildings. Follow the well-defined track leading down to the farm. The farmer is aware that people will be walking through his farmyard, and is quite happy about it. Do take extra care not to disturb any cattle or sheep, and ensure that all gates are closed. Gaining the Williamscot road (point D), turn left. A short distance further on one will emerge on to the Williamscot to Cropredy road. Then turn to the left, passing the entrance to Williamscot House (Pathfinder 1022 479457) on the homeward route.

Crossing over Cropredy Bridge, pause to view the stone memorial set in the wall. For a clear view of the structure, one may walk down into the playing fields just before the bridge, via a concrete path. A small gate barring the way into the fields bears a sign prohibiting dogs. Scale the gate and note that a path is being beaten along the river bank – another right of way in the making. After viewing the bridge, return to the road and to the starting point at the Bridge Stores.

Continue past the starting point and on to the canal, down to the tow-path once more, only on this occasion, turn to the right. Walk along to the next bridge and, passing beneath it, turn sharp right and walk through a gate to emerge at the end of Red Lion Street. Walk up the road, with the church on the left. To the right is the Red Lion, where refreshment may be taken.

Emerging from the Red Lion, walk over to the church of St Mary the Virgin, gaining access via the iron gate at the end of the road. Walk through the churchyard and around to the other side, where entry can be effected. Inside, there is a brass lectern with a globe on which rests a glittering eagle. During the conflict, there were fears among the congregation that the lectern would be destroyed by the Roundheads, and so it was lowered into the Cherwell. Some years on, it was recovered (with difficulty, having sunk into the mud) and replaced. One of its three brass feet was gone, so another foot, of bronze, was fashioned as a replacement. For many years, the church has displayed armour and other relics of the 1644 battle. Sadly some items have been stolen, but others remain.

Leaving the church, turn left at the top of Red Lion Street. Walking on, one returns to the road leading to the Bridge Stores.

# *Further Explorations*

Cropredy is an interesting village in which to linger. Originally, it was held by the Bishop of Lincoln, from whence it passed through several hands, including those of Edward VI until, in the late eighteenth century, it was sold off to Brasenose College, Oxford. In the High Street, there stands a house which was owned by a carter, who went out of business when the canal was constructed. The canal, in turn, was supplanted by the coming of the railway, in 1850. Finally, the resurgence of road transport closed the railway – and the wheel had turned full circle.

The nearest town is Banbury, 4 miles to the south. Of Saxon origin, this small town was an important settlement long before many of today's urban sprawls were glints in their founders' eyes. It figures in the Wars of the Roses, notably in the run-up to the Battle of Edgcote, but assumed a more significant role in the Civil War because of its position in relation to Royalist Oxford. A strong Parliamentary garrison could seriously hamper communications between the Royalist capital and the north. Charles took the town soon after Edgehill. Banbury Castle was held by almost one thousand Parliamentarian troops, but surrendered with unseemly haste as soon as the Royalists opened fire. From this time, its defence was high on the list of Royalist priorities and in 1644, it withstood a lengthy siege.

The siege began in earnest on 25 August 1644, when Roundhead infantry actually penetrated the town, aiming for a quick knock-out blow. When this failed, the Royalist commander was called upon to surrender, but morale (of the garrison, if not the townsfolk) remained high despite the threat of an investing force of some three thousand five hundred troops, supported by heavy artillery. The siege then settled down into a well-worn pattern, with a continuous artillery barrage punctuated by occasional adventurous forays by the Royalist garrison. Efforts at mining the castle walls came to nothing when underground streams flooded the tunnels dug by the Roundhead engineers. An outbreak of plague within the town accounted for most of the deaths. Eventually, the siege was raised by the Earl of Northampton, who relieved the garrison on 25 October.

It is said that to prevent a recurrence of the suffering they had endured during the Civil War, the citizens of Banbury pulled down the castle, in the hope of reducing the town's value in any future civil conflict. Trials of those suspected of having Royalist sympathies were held in Banbury after the cessation of hostilities. Cromwell presided at trials held in the Reindeer public house and the ghost of a cavalier, possibly one of the condemned victims of this witch-hunt, is said to haunt the place to this day.

A little to the north-east of Cropredy is Chipping Warden, less than a mile from Edgcote – Edgcote House itself can be seen from the church tower. Lying to the left of the A361 as you approach Chipping Warden from the south is Arbury Hill (Pathfinder 1022 494486), the site of an Iron Age fort, occupied around 600 BC. Almost adjacent to Arbury Hill is Chipping Warden Airfield (Pathfinder 1022 495496), home to Wellington bombers from 1941 to 1945. Thus, the area has had continued military significance for a period in excess of thirteen hundred years.

Down the A361 towards Wardington is Hay's Bridge (Pathfinder 1022 488476), to the north of which Charles managed to turn his vanguard and march to Cleveland's aid. Hay's Bridge has not been included in the walk because the A361 is not recommended for rambling, being a very busy road and having little in the way of grass verge.

Wardington (Pathfinder 1022 491465) has already been mentioned in connection with the Battle of Edgcote. The Jacobean manor-house (493461) can be glimpsed through wrought-iron gates, and the church of St Mary Magdalene (491465) contains an unusual medieval slab in the floor, depicting a man's head, with hands clasped in prayer.

## *Further Information*

Cropredy nestles between the A361 Banbury to Daventry road and the A423 Banbury to Coventry road and, as such, is quite accessible by car. As in several instances in this book, the M40 has led to much-improved communications.

For access by British Rail via Banbury, telephone (0295) 262256. For National Express coach information, telephone (0865) 791579.

Ordnance Survey maps for the area are Landranger 151 and Pathfinder 1022. Further reading is provided by Margaret Toynbee and Peter Young's *Cropredy Bridge, 1644: The Campaign and the Battle* (Roundwood Press, 1970).

# 12
# THE BATTLE OF NASEBY
## 14 June 1645

## *The Road to Naseby*

By March 1645 Charles was in despondent mood. He had been engaged in peace negotiations at Uxbridge which had led to nothing – probably because he had been angling for the opposing armies to be disbanded before continuing discussions. In 1644 he had called a Parliament of his own supporters in Oxford, but had found this as little to his liking as the real thing at Westminster. In February 1645, Shrewsbury – a significant town in terms of communications with Royalist Wales – had fallen.

By the end of March, however, Charles had regained sufficient resolution to consider marching north to attack the depleted Scottish army encamped in Yorkshire, but he was prevented from doing so by Cromwell who, with fifteen hundred men, set off himself to harass the countryside around Oxford.

On 7 May, Charles marched out of Oxford to Stow-on-the-Wold, where he chaired a conference called specifically to discuss possible action in view of the present circumstances. He learned that Fairfax and the New Model Army were marching west to relieve Taunton, which meant that the only substantial Parliamentarian forces to the north were those laying siege to Chester, and the Scottish army, which was now besieging Pontefract. Prince Rupert proposed a march north, to relieve Chester, overthrow the Scots and establish communications with Montrose, who was continuing to do well in Scotland.

Other advisers, notably Lord Digby, pressed for an immediate attack on Fairfax and the New Model Army. Charles decided on a compromise and in doing so committed a fatal error – he split his force. George Goring was sent west to capture Taunton and subdue the New Model Army while, accompanied by Rupert, Charles himself would go north. Unfortunately Fairfax had received orders to return to Oxfordshire to lend weight to Cromwell's investment of Oxford.

Charles's indecisiveness often worked in his favour, for how could his enemies predict his next move when he did not know himself? If pressure was put on Oxford, the king would, it was felt, give priority to its protection and not march anywhere at all. Messengers were dispatched to instruct Goring to return from the west and ride to the royal capital's relief. However, Rupert proposed that the surest manner of drawing Fairfax from Oxford was to attack a Parliamentary stronghold. And so Charles determined to lay siege to Leicester. Formal notice of this intent was given to the citizens of Leicester on 30 May. By the end of the day, Leicester had been taken and the town sacked. Charles remained in the city until Sunday 1 June when he decided to return south to the relief of Oxford. By the time he reached Market Harborough, however, he had changed his mind again, determining not to ride to the relief of Oxford (which did not appear to be in much danger from Fairfax) but merely to send a convoy of provisions accompanied by a force of twelve hundred cavalry to fortify the garrison. He remained in Daventry for almost a week, awaiting the return of the escort. Meanwhile, Fairfax had been given a free hand to prosecute the war against the king as he thought fit, and had marched to Kislingbury, only 10 miles east of Daventry, where he was joined by Cromwell with six or seven hundred troopers from East Anglia, where the latter had been dispatched in the event of the king deciding to ride east.

On the morning of 13 June, Charles moved out of Daventry, bound once more for Market Harborough, without realizing that Fairfax was only 10 miles away. Fairfax, resolving to remain hot on the heels of his quarry, pulled out of Kislingbury to shadow the king. Charles' army was well spread out, Rupert spending the night of 13 June in Market Harborough, while Charles himself slept in Lubbenham, 2 miles to the west. Part of the Royalist rearguard was in Naseby village, where they were captured, playing darts in a local inn, by an advance Roundhead party commanded by Colonel Henry Ireton.

When this intelligence reached Charles, he had to decide whether to push north to Leicester in the hope of picking up further recruits or to give battle. His military advisers, including Rupert, were of the opinion that it would be wiser to avoid a confrontation at this juncture, but Digby and the courtiers convinced Charles that he should stand and fight. And so, in the early hours of 14 June, the Royalist army prepared to move south, to meet Fairfax to the north-west of Naseby village.

## *The Battle of Naseby*

As the Royalist army were preparing to move out, Fairfax himself pulled out of Guilsborough with the objective of harrying the supposed Royalist march north and eventually forcing a battle at a propitious moment. Perceiving this strategy, even Rupert saw that there was now little option but to stand and fight. If he did so, then he could contrive to choose his ground and possibly introduce an element of surprise. The cat and mouse tactics employed by Fairfax would hardly permit the launch of an attack on the very defendable Royalist ridge below Market Harborough, and so Rupert located a similarly advantageous position closer to the Roundhead lines, from which an offensive could be launched. This was at Dust Hill, a ridge 1½ miles to the north of Naseby, the main concern now being that the New Model Army was much better prepared than he had expected.

The Royalists drew up along Dust Hill. Langdale's northern horse was on the Royalist left, stretching out towards the Naseby to Clipston road, while Rupert's cavalry took pride of place on the right wing. Sandwiched between was Astley's body of foot. The Roundhead army was initially thinly deployed on a wide front from Sulby to the Naseby to Kelmarsh road. Cromwell commanded the horse on the right wing, with Ireton on the left and Major-General Philip Skippon's foot facing Astley in the centre. Modifications to the Roundhead order included a line of dragoons under Colonel Oakey, concealed behind a hedge on the extreme left, and some three hundred musketeers positioned well to the fore of the infantry line.

Numerically, Fairfax enjoyed the advantage. Indeed, it has often been claimed that Roundheads outnumbered Royalists by two to one. Such superiority is unlikely. Standard New Model organization renders it feasible

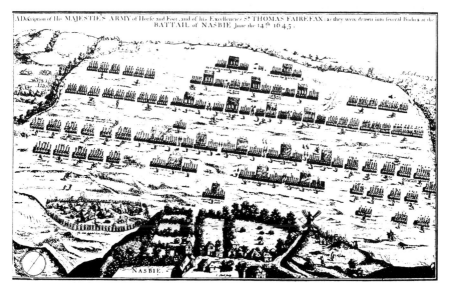

The Battle of Naseby, as depicted in Joshua Sprigge's *Anglia Rediviva* (1647)

to hazard an estimate of something in excess of fourteen thousand Parliamentarians, split fairly evenly between horse and foot. Royalist numbers are more difficult to assess, the lowest estimate being seven thousand five hundred, the highest twelve thousand. As is customary in such matters, the truth probably lies somewhere between the two extremes.

Whatever the Royalists lacked in numbers, they more than compensated for in experience and enthusiasm, personified in Rupert's irresistible panache and the indefatigable resolution of Jacob Astley. The New Model Army, on the other hand, comprised many raw recruits, and by his deployment of dragoons and musketeers, Fairfax must have hoped to take the edge off the fearsome prospect of a combined Royalist cavalry charge and relentless foot advance.

Shortly before ten o'clock, Fairfax drew Skippon's foot back from view and it is sometimes argued that Rupert, duped into thinking that a full retreat was under way, embarked upon a premature advance. However, having determined to give battle, there would have been little to gain by further delay, and Rupert's cavalry charge was the opening gambit of the engagement. Colonel Oakey subsequently claimed a leading role in the conflict, insisting that much of the sting was taken out of Rupert's onslaught by the concentrated firepower of his dragoons.

In fact, firepower played a very minor and largely ineffective role in the battle. Parliamentary artillery fire did no damage at all and there is little evidence to suggest that the dragoons inflicted many casualties on Rupert's cavalry as it contemptuously swept aside the extreme left of Ireton's horse. Towards the centre, the Roundheads fared rather better, Prince Maurice's contingent of horse being beaten back.

Astley's infantry, striding out purposefully, soon encountered Skippon's line. Skippon himself was wounded by a musket ball and although he refused to leave the field, his men were none the less deprived of effective leadership. Although Astley tried to press home his advantage, Ireton, conscious of the imminent collapse of the Roundhead foot, personally led a charge on Astley's right flank in a gallant attempt to relieve the pressure. In the process, he himself was wounded and temporarily taken prisoner.

Meanwhile, the victorious Rupert, as at Edgehill three years before, was unable to rally his men who charged on through the Parliamentarian lines as far as Naseby, where they attempted to take the enemy baggage train. This they were unable to accomplish for it was well guarded by musketeers. Unfortunately for the Royalist cause, the efforts of Rupert on the right and Astley in the centre were not matched by the performance of Langdale's northern horse on the left. True, Langdale suffered from the disadvantage of having to advance uphill to meet Cromwell's downhill charge, but it is nevertheless tempting to suggest that his commitment was not comparable with that of his colleagues. It should perhaps be remembered that it had been his preference to march north, and in seventeenth-century England, campaigns in the south and Midlands must have been tantamount to fighting overseas as far as the parochially-minded Yorkshiremen were concerned. In any event, the Roundhead success against Langdale was to turn the tide of battle.

The outcome was also determined by the respective sides' use of reserves, Roundhead reserves being used expediently. With Astley's foot holding its own in the centre, for example, Fairfax introduced three regiments from his reserve which helped to drive back, by sheer weight of numbers, the Royalist infantry, tiring after an hour's fighting without succour. And to insure against the possibility of Langdale falling back and regrouping, Cromwell committed two regiments of horse to outflank him. The Royalist reserve, meanwhile, remained immovable on Dust Hill, awaiting informed direction. This was likely to emanate only from Rupert, who was wasting valuable time laying siege to the Roundhead baggage train. Ultimately, Rupert did succeed in rallying his men and returning to the field of battle, by which time the outcome had already been determined. The *coup de grâce* to Astley's infantry was delivered jointly by Oakey's dragoons, who, emerging from cover, assaulted the Royalist right, and by Ireton, now back in the saddle, who manoeuvred to attack from the left.

In such a situation, there was very little Rupert could do. Again, as at Edgehill, his horses were too exhausted for the launching of a relief action and so, instead of riding to the hard-pressed Astley's aid, he returned to the king's side where, together, they watched the systematic destruction of their gallant infantry, which surely fought on in the expectation of forthcoming cavalry support. The Royalist reserves may not have numbered much above one thousand men – certainly far below the strength of Fairfax's reserve – yet a thousand fresh troops could have achieved much if used to bolster the collapsing infantry lines. The fact is that the king was beaten and the defeat was about to develop into a rout. In such circumstances, the retreating foot would have stood very little chance of survival. Better, perhaps, to think ahead, retaining the reserve intact, together with Rupert's cavalry, even if it meant watching the stout-hearted Astley and his infantry being cut to pieces.

This plan did involve maintaining discipline within the ranks and, as observed time and again, military discipline was not high on the list of Royalist priorities. An incident, insignificant in itself, compounded the error. The king, inclined, apparently, towards a last-ditch attempt to save the day, placed himself at the head of his own lifeguard as if in the act of spearheading one final charge. He was stopped by the Earl of Carnwath who, impelled no doubt by the best of motives, took hold of his bridle and, with a curse upon his lips, said 'Will you go upon your death in an instant?' In so doing, he turned the king's horse around to the right, away from the fighting. The reserve, growing increasingly agitated at the Royal indecisiveness in such desperate circumstances, interpreted the manoeuvre as a signal that the day was lost. In obeisance to what they took to be an order to retreat, they turned upon their heels (many, no doubt, a little too eagerly) and fled the field. Many military historians have censured Carnwath for his action, yet he can hardly be faulted for trying to keep his sovereign alive. With the king dead or captured, all would most certainly be lost. Better, then, to stand off in the hope of having the strength to fight another day. The preservation of the Royal Person and the retention of his powers were, after all, the avowed aims of the men who were laying down their lives that very day, and it may be unfair to blame what was in essence a noble action for the shameful retreat of an ill-disciplined and inadequately led army.

An organized rearguard action was out of the question as every man sought to save his own skin, a situation of which the pursuing Roundheads took full advantage, harrying the fleeing Royalists to Great Glen, 2 miles short of Leicester.

## *The Aftermath*

The short-term results of the Naseby action were severe enough for the Royalists – a seasoned army routed, its courage and resolution destroyed. On the king's side, casualties probably amounted to around one thousand dead, including those slain in the long flight to Leicester, and one hundred or so camp followers deserted by their beaux and mercilessly butchered by the more zealous Parliamentarians. Five thousand prisoners were also taken, making Charles a commander without an army, the bulk of the prisoners being battle-hardened foot-soldiers, whom it would be impossible to replace. Similarly, at a time when the Royalists were importing arms from the Netherlands at twice the cost of London and Midlands-manufactured Roundhead weaponry, they could ill afford the loss of their artillery and some eight thousand arms. Plunder from the sacking of Leicester also fell into the hands of the Roundhead rank and file where, despite the protestations of the citizens, it remained.

In the long term, and although Charles himself tried to make light of it, the loss of the royal private papers, which had been with the baggage train, did much to harm the royal cause. Parliament, quick to appreciate their propaganda value, soon had pamphlets out on the streets. Consisting in part of copies of letters to the queen, the incriminating documents dealt with plans to bring French mercenaries to England and, worse still, to solicit the services of discontented Irish Catholics with the promise of a repeal of the recusancy laws, which made attendance at Anglican services compulsory. To regain his throne, the king would clearly stop at nothing.

From Leicester, Charles repaired to Hereford and, from there, to South Wales. It was from Wales and the West Country that he might have mounted one last offensive at the head of a new army comprising the Naseby survivors and Goring's seven thousand men still besieging Taunton. But, again, he wavered, idling away four crucial weeks at Raglan Castle before embarking on a further series of aimless perambulations.

On the other hand, Naseby proved the making of the New Model Army, which now went from strength to strength. Although experienced cavalry had contributed greatly to the Parliamentary success, the foot gained precious experience, and the invaluable confidence which accompanies the defeat of formidable opponents. Of the battle, Cromwell himself said, 'When I saw the enemy draw up and march in gallant order towards us, and we a company of poor ignorant men . . . I could not . . . but smile out to God in praises, in assurance of victory.' Perhaps his trust in God had been strengthened somewhat by the knowledge that the Royalists were so obviously outnumbered. Even so, credit cannot be taken away from the efficiency of the New Model Army, which now, disturbingly, began to distance itself from its Parliamentary masters.

Naseby is traditionally and fairly described as the decisive battle of the English Civil War but, in the search for answers as to why the Royalists lost the war, their defeat on 14 June 1645 must rank as a symptom of deeper root causes, it being doubtful whether Charles had the ability to win under any circumstances. Sooner or later, in outcome if not in name, he would have met his Naseby.

# *Walk One*

**Distance:**   7½ miles (12 km)

Naseby has a museum devoted largely to the battle. Open from Easter to the end of September, on Sundays and Bank Holidays from 2.00 to 5.00 p.m., the museum is essentially a friendly, family concern, and stands at the corner of Calendar Lane (Pathfinder 957 688775). It is easily found by following the tourist signposts. Start from the museum car-park (point A), which is usually situated in a clearly marked field but which, in wet weather, may be on the garage forecourt immediately in front of the museum. A better idea of the lie of the land will be acquired by visiting the museum before starting out.

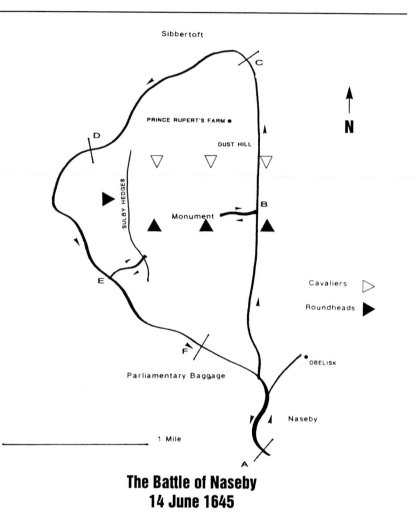

Sibbertoft

PRINCE RUPERT'S FARM •

DUST HILL

N

D

SULBY HEDGES

Monument

B

E

Cavaliers

Roundheads

F

Parliamentary Baggage

OBELISK

Naseby

1 Mile

A

## The Battle of Naseby
## 14 June 1645

Emerging from the museum, turn left as if to walk into the village. At the junction, walk over to Nutcote, a road lined with new houses. Bear right up towards Church Street. The Royal Oak is on the left. Keep on, past the Fitzgerald Arms, and turn left on the Welford Road. A little way down on the right is the road to Sibbertoft. Turn here because this is the road which runs through the centre of the battlefield.

If the A1–M1 link road has not been completed (it is due to be in February 1994), then a straight road is ahead. If it has been completed, then shortly after turning, a little overpass on the right-hand side of the old road takes one safely over it. Returning to the old road walk up to Mill Hill and the Roundhead rear. Cromwell would have moved in from the right.

Continue until reaching the sign indicating a small track leading off to the battlefield monument on the left. Walk down to the monument (Pathfinder 937 686803) (point B), which provides a useful pictorial representation of the deployment of both armies. Roundheads lined this ridge. In the distance, the Royalists were drawn up on Dust Hill – between both armies a slight dip. Roundhead dragoons occupied Sulby Hedges on the far left.

Return to the road and continue walking towards Sibbertoft. Fairfax dispatched a band of musketeers to the foot of the slope facing the enemy advance. The Royalists took the fight to the enemy by advancing into the dip, and then uphill. Walk on to the junction with the Sibbertoft to Kelmarsh road (point C). The Royalists marched in from the right, but turn left towards Sibbertoft.

A sharp right-hand bend in the road leads into Sibbertoft. At this bend, off to the left, look for a bridle-way sign. Follow the sign along the farm track. The bridle-way is marked by arrows – but keep a sharp look-out for them. Turn sharp right at the farm building. At the end of the field, look to the right for a few strips of concrete – an indication of the old Sibbertoft Airfield. Follow the track around to the left and leave it by branching off to the right through the fields. The drain on the left keeps one on the straight and narrow. At the end of the drain, a 'Private' sign looms up on the right, but opposite is the continuation of the bridle-way.

According to the Pathfinder 937, the bridle-way runs diagonally across the fields. In fact it has been diverted to follow the field boundaries. The farmer has left hardly sufficient width for a bridle-way, with the result that riders have strayed on to cultivated land. The going is rather difficult in wet weather and a lost horseshoe may even be encountered. Once again, horseshoe tracks help to mark the path. One gradually approaches a tract of woodland, which looms up as, continuing to follow the field perimeters, one finds another farm track on the left. Walking parallel with this track, the going is made a little easier if one is able to leap the ditch on the left and continue along the track until reaching the ruins of another farm building (point D).

Hugging the hedgerow, past the building, one reaches the end of the field. The wood is now ahead. Walk diagonally across the field to the left towards a small gate leading into the wood. Take the path through the centre of the wood. Paths through woods are invariably muddy because they can rarely dry out. When one emerges at the other side, the bridle-way becomes a grass pathway, leading straight on to the Welford road. As one walks down this path, look to the left over the fields towards Sulby Hedges where the Roundhead dragoons were hidden.

Turn left on to the Welford road (Pathfinder 937 661884), in the direction of Naseby. Just before reaching the lodge leading to Naseby Hall on the right, one can take a detour on a track off to the left (point E), which leads to the 1645 site of Sulby Hedges. Walking down into Naseby, depending once again upon the timing of one's visit, one may have to negotiate another overpass. Descending from it, one is directly in the line of Prince Rupert's assault on the Roundhead baggage train lying over the fields to the right (point F). Continuing into Naseby, turn right into Church Street and take refreshment at either the Fitzgerald Arms or the Royal Oak.

An alternative return route is provided by turning right at the top of Sibbertoft Road. This runs down towards Clipston and along the Royalist route to the battlefield. (While walking downhill, remember that the Royalists were marching uphill, with full kit.) Reaching the Clipston crossroads, turn right along the B4036, towards Naseby. Glance to the right and note that the centre of the action is shielded by Naseby Covert.

Eventually, a track off to the left (leading to Kelmarsh) by New House Farm gives the position of Cromwell's approach to the battlefield. Note that the ground is low lying and heavy. At New House Farm, cross over the new road. Shortly after descending to the old road, the Fitzgerald Obelisk (Pathfinder 957 694784), enshrouded in trees, looms up on the left. Erected in 1823 by John and Mary Fitzgerald, Lord and Lady of the Manor of Naseby, it seems strangely distant from the action. Entering Naseby, turn to the left, down Haselbech Road and a little way up, on the right, there is a public footpath sign. Negotiate the stile and follow the hedgerow – the church is on the right. Go through into the next field. At a walkers' signpost, take the Cottesbrooke path through a copse and emerge (via a broken stile) into a field. Walk over the field towards the gate ahead, emerging on to Calendar Lane. The museum is on the other side of the road.

Apart from the final section through the fields, this route is exclusively tarmac. Road walking used to be quite popular, but due to the danger posed by increased traffic, its desirability has declined. One has to be quite nimble on one's feet and when satisfactory grass verges are lacking, much attention has to be allocated to watching and listening for the approach of traffic from front and rear.

# *Walk Two*

A village walk of about 1¼ miles (2 km), providing an aperitif to the main battlefield course, or a less invigorating alternative for the unseasoned rambler, might take the following form.

Begin at the museum (Pathfinder 957 688775), turning left on to Calendar Lane. At the junction, bear right and walk up towards the High Street. On the right, is the thatched Catton Cottage, one of two remaining seventeenth-century cottages in Naseby. Continue up to School Lane, at the far corner of which is Cromwell Cottage, the other surviving cottage contemporary with the battle. At the top of the High Street, turn left into Newlands, at the other end of which is the church of All Saints.

The present building dates from the thirteenth century, although it has a Saxon predecessor. Hanging on one of the walls are a sword and a stirrup, found on the battlefield. There were two swords until June 1992, when one was stolen. The most curious relic, however, is Cromwell's Table, standing by the north door. The inn at which the Cavaliers were surprised by the Roundheads on the eve of the battle stood opposite the church on the site of Shuckburgh House (built in 1773) and legend has it that the Cavaliers were seated at this table when captured. A variation on this story has Cromwell supping at it after the battle. Apparently, at the turn of the present century, the table was spotted in the back yard of Shuckburgh House, very much the worse for wear. The then rector of Naseby, receiving permission to remove it, had it restored and it has resided in the church ever since.

Coming out of the church, turn left into Church Street and walk past the war memorial to Carvells Lane (Pathfinder 957 687779), branching off to the right. Turn into Carvells Lane and walk along a rough track which has remained essentially unchanged for centuries. The Parliamentary baggage train occupied a substantial area in the fields to the right. The track is straight and slightly undulating and, walking along, one feels that if one continued to the end, one would be sure to emerge into the seventeenth century.

When ready to return to the present day, retrace your steps and turn right into Church Street. The Royal Oak stands invitingly on the next corner. Continue along Church Street, past the Cold Ashby road into Nutcote, at the end of which is Calendar Lane opposite, with the museum, the starting point, on the corner.

Walking through the village, it is easy to picture the effects of the battle upon the lives of the villagers, secreting valuables for fear of pillage by the winning side. Small hoards of coins are still dug up in the fields, and one wonders how many valuable potential finds will be lost for ever beneath the tarmac of the new road.

# *Further Explorations*

Northamptonshire is a county rich in Civil War associations. While the towns (with the exception of Towcester) supported Parliament, the landed gentry were for king and country. Charles II repaid Northampton's disloyalty by having Northampton Castle demolished. However, the town had reaped a much greater reward through its support of the Parliamentary cause with the placement of considerable orders for army boots – and so began the world famous Northamptonshire boot and shoe industry.

Royalist headquarters in the county were at Holdenby House (Landranger 152 6867). It was here that Charles was held prisoner for five months. Built by Sir Christopher Hatton in 1583, it was once one of the largest houses in England. At the time of the Civil War, it belonged to the Crown but, following the king's execution, it was sold to a Parliamentarian, Adam Baynes, who demolished it all save for the small part remaining today. A small museum houses Civil War relics. Museum, house and gardens (where one may literally follow in Charles I's footsteps) are open in the afternoons from April to the end of September. Telephone (0604) 770074 for further details.

One of the most curious stories of the Civil War concerns the Wheatsheaf Inn in Daventry (Landranger 152 5662), where Charles I lodged before Naseby. During the course of two nights of disturbed sleep, the king's troubled mind, perhaps conscious of the imminence of a decisive battle, conjured up the appearance of the Earl of Strafford, sacrificed four years earlier to appease his master's critics. Carrying his loyalty to Charles beyond the grave (and, some would say, a little too far in view of the unfortunate circumstances of his demise), the earl's apparition spoke, warning the king to defer any engagement with Roundhead forces. Hearing Charles's voice, his attendants burst into his bedchamber to find him alone and in a bewildered, dishevelled state. Pale and perspiring, he dismissed it all as a frightful dream. The following night, however, the phantom earl came again, on this occasion more vehement in his demands that the king should tarry no longer in Northamptonshire. Although Charles again made light of the incident (which, doubtless, has been generously embellished in the telling and retelling), it cannot have helped to bolster the vacillating monarch's failing resolution.

Northampton is also worth a visit. The town itself was the scene of a significant Roses battle in July 1460. The decision – a Yorkist victory for Prince Edward and Warwick against Queen Margaret and Henry VI – was reversed only five months later at Wakefield. Unfortunately the battlefield has long since been rendered unrecognizable by modern day developments.

All that remains of Northampton Castle is the Postern Gate, incorporated into the railway station (Landranger 152 7460). Northamptonshire folk have never regretted its loss. As one chronicler put it, 'It is better to make boots and shoes than to be the shuttle-feathers of tyrannic monarchs.' Medieval Parliaments once sat in Northampton Castle, and Thomas à Becket was tried there, but all Northamptonshire folk seem to care for are boots and shoes, and there is certainly no shortage of boot and shoe and leathercraft collections, a curious footnote for a county which likes to be known for its 'spires and squires'.

# Further Information

After the completion of the A1–M1 link road, the battlefield should be easily accessible from all directions – north and south via the M1, west via the M6 and east via the A1–M1 link. Naseby itself is perched midway between the A50 Leicester to Northampton road and the A508 Market Harborough to Northampton road.

Travellers by British Rail should make for Kettering (tel: (0533) 629811) on the St Pancras Line or Northampton (tel: (0788) 560116) on the Euston Line. For National Express coach details, telephone 021 622 4373, and for local bus connections, telephone United Counties (0536) 512411.

Ordnance Survey maps for the area are Landrangers 141 and 152, and Pathfinders 937 and 957. Further reading is provided by two books. Peter Young's *Naseby 1645: The Campaign and the Battle* (Century, 1985) should be the definitive volume. Originally intended to follow on from the superb *Edgehill* and *Marston Moor* volumes from the Roundwood Press, publishing difficulties led to it not being illustrated at all – a severe limitation on a book about battles. Happily, this book can now be supplemented with *The Battle of Naseby* by Maurice Ashley (Alan Sutton Publishing, 1992), and *Naseby Fight 1645* by B. Denton (Partizan Press, 4th ed., 1991).

# 13
# THE SIEGE OF NEWARK
## 26 November 1645 to 8 May 1646

## *The Road to Newark*

The strategic importance of Newark in troubled times had been brought home to its citizens when the final throw of the Yorkist dice led to two opposing armies converging on the town in 1487. Then, the ensuing battle had taken place 4 miles to the south, at East Stoke. But, in 1642, if the town had hoped to stand on the sidelines during a long and bloody Civil War, then it was to be bitterly disappointed.

During the period 1643–6, Newark was under siege on three occasions: 27–9 February 1643, 29 February–21 March 1644 and 26 November 1645–8 May 1646. The town's advantageous position was appreciated by both sides from the outset, but the sympathies of the influential citizens were with the king and Newark became a Royalist stronghold, a counter to the Parliamentary garrisons at Lincoln and Nottingham, and a valuable link with the east coast ports.

Initially, the Newark garrison comprised fifteen hundred men under the command of the Royal Governor, Sir John Henderson, who set to work at once to improve the town defences by constructing an earthen rampart bordered by a dry ditch. Crude it might have seemed, but the work reflected the latest European techniques in siege warfare, which Henderson himself had gleaned from visits abroad. In any event, the new defences extended only to the south-west, excluding both Northgate and Millgate, the governor having no intention of spreading his meagre forces too thinly.

What has come to be known as the First Siege was, in fact, little more than a precipitate, though determined, Parliamentarian assault. On learning that Major-General Thomas Ballard intended launching an assault on the town from his base at Buckingham, Henderson attempted to forestall the plan by making a surprise attack on the Parliamentarian position. The Roundheads were on the alert, however, and Henderson found it prudent to withdraw. So Ballard launched his assault as planned, on 27 February 1643.

At the head of six thousand men and with ten pieces of artillery, the Parliamentary commander was confident of success. The besieged, who had taken up a defensive position due east of the town, on Beacon Hill, fell back as the Roundheads advanced. Ballard called for the town's surrender. Henderson refused.

Ballard ordered a bombardment, under cover of which troops were dispatched with orders to take the Spittle (the site of the medieval Hospital of St Leonard). Henderson, foreseeing such a move, had arranged for all Northgate, where the Spittle lay, to be burned to the ground. The battle for the town raged throughout the day with the besiegers taking the remains of the Spittle, from where they were able to launch a direct assault on the earthworks. Although beaten back, the Royalists rallied and mounted a counter-attack, over-running the Roundhead forward positions to force a withdrawal.

Despite the enthusiasm of his captains for a renewed assault on 28 February, Ballard insisted on withdrawing. There were those who attributed the major-general's reluctance to his concern for friends trapped in the town, but the truth was that the Roundheads had suffered heavy losses – some two hundred dead against a handful of Royalist casualties, a pattern which was likely to be repeated if the offensive was maintained. And so ended the first siege of Newark.

Newark was not seriously threatened again for exactly one year, the tide of battle in the East Midlands having swung first to the Royalists and then in

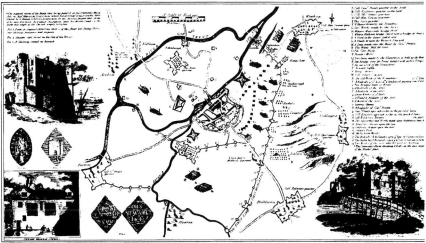

Detail from Richard Clampe's Siege Plan. Clampe was an engineer with the besieging Parliamentary army (Nottingham County Council Leisure Services)

favour of Parliament. Until the Autumn of 1643, when the town moved back on to the defensive, the garrison played a role in attacks on Parliamentarian Grantham and Nottingham. Royalist reverses occurring during the latter part of 1643 were blamed on Sir John Henderson, whose stubborn defence of Newark was forgotten. Henderson was replaced by Sir Richard Byron, one of a family of fighting Royalists.

On 29 February 1644, Sir John Meldrum invested Newark with a force of seven thousand men and heavy artillery. Meldrum was a great believer in the continuous artillery barrage and at once commenced a relentless round of cannon and mortar fire. On 6 March, he attacked Muskham Bridge and took the Royalist redoubt, setting up his field headquarters opposite the bridge in the Spittle ruins. The second siege was clearly going much better for Parliament than the first. This time, the defenders were too weak to give consideration to mounting a counter-attack and it seemed only a matter of time before the town fell.

If the siege were to be lifted, then outside help would be required. The regional Royalist Commander, Lord Loughborough, with only three thousand men to put into the field, lacked the muscle to dislodge Meldrum and so an urgent appeal was made to the king. The job fell to a reluctant Prince Rupert who, by mid-March, had cobbled together a force of sufficient strength to challenge the besiegers. His arrival on the morning of 21 March, on Beacon Hill, caught Meldrum unawares. The latter was now faced with the besieger's nightmare of being caught between the defending garrison and the relief column. Consolidating his position in the Spittle, he sent a body of horse to advance on Beacon Hill. If he hoped that this would halt Rupert's progress, then he obviously did not know his prince. At 9.00 a.m., Rupert charged through the Roundhead cavalry, which fell back to the Spittle. When Byron, at the head of the Royalist garrison, sallied forth, Meldrum, at risk of being wiped out by the multi-pronged attack, surrendered, and on 22 March he was allowed to quit the theatre of operations, less 200 casualties, 3,000 muskets, 11 cannon and 2 mortars.

For the Royalists, this was a famous victory, the Roundhead garrison at Lincoln, in fear of imminent attack, abandoning ship, while Nottingham and Derby made ready to repel boarders.

# *The Great Siege of Newark*

The initial battles for Newark scarcely merit the term 'siege'. The first lasted only a day, while the duration of the second was three weeks. But the third siege, *the* siege of Newark, was not resolved until it had entered its sixth month.

A remarkably well-preserved portion of the earthwork known as The Queen's Sconce

The actions of 1643 and 1644 had exposed weaknesses in the town defences – weaknesses which the Royalists sought to rectify. After 1644, two important works were undertaken – the King's Sconce and the Queen's Sconce, substantial earthworks which were really makeshift forts. The latter was constructed to protect the southern approaches to the town while the former, to the north, occupied the site of the Spittle buildings.

By 1645, Byron had been replaced as governor by Sir Richard Willys, the third of the royal appointees. Like Henderson, Byron had been dismissed following a minor defeat, his past triumphs being forgotten by an unforgiving royal master. The last great battle of the Civil War had been fought at Naseby in June, and yet Charles resolved to fight on – to the last drop of his supporters' blood if necessary. In fact, most of them had been bled dry, once prosperous families having reduced themselves to penury in support of the royal cause.

As it turned out, declining Royalist fortunes worked in Newark's favour. Although the town now stood alone as the last bastion of Royalist resistance in eastern England, the diehard monarchists, having nowhere else to go, flocked to the gates. Even Charles was forced to seek sanctuary within its walls. After what remained of his army had been severely mauled at Rowton Heath, he made a break for Newark, arriving safely on 4 October. During his stay at Newark, Prince Rupert (with the compliance of Willys), forced his way into his uncle's presence, and Charles was persuaded to publish a partial vindication of Rupert's action in surrendering Bristol. With the approach of the Scots army under the command of General Leslie, both Royals took their leave of the town, Charles having vented his spleen on Willys by replacing him with Lord John Belasyse, Commander of the Royal Horse Guard.

On 26 November 1645, Leslie arrived at the outskirts of the town and, meeting little resistance, immediately took Muskham Bridge. Belasyse, stocked up with provisions, busied himself by establishing a mint to produce siege coinage, and sat tight. While the Scots constructed their own redoubt between the town and the river, Colonel Rossiter and General Poyntz (a late entrant to the war, but a valuable one, having seen service as a mercenary in Germany and the Netherlands) established themselves in the surrounding villages, where they proceeded to build more earthworks.

Despite all this activity with picks and shovels, the cordon thrown around the town was a loose one and supplies were still getting through. In an attempt to close the loopholes, Poyntz constructed a 'line of circum-navigation', a Maginot Line of sorts, comprising a chain of earthworks, joined by earthen ramparts and stretching from Crankley Point to the river, south of Hawton. This rambling edifice was subsequently strengthened by being dissected at Beacon Hill, a second line being added well to the north of Hawton and to the south of the Queen's Sconce.

By March 1646, following four months' intense preparation by both sides, the siege began in earnest, with Poyntz determined to starve Newark into submission. In addition to subjecting the town to a continuous barrage from his big guns, positioned along the earthwork chain, he conceived the dastardly scheme of damming the Trent and the Devon to ensure that Newark was deprived of water power and, ultimately, of water itself. Food stocks decreased, but by far the greatest enemy, as in any siege situation, was disease and the inevitable outbreak of plague. At least two hundred were to die, interred in mass graves. And yet, despite their suffering, the defenders were still full of fight, mounting sorties into enemy-held territory.

Nevertheless, on 28 March 1646, Poyntz considered Newark's position so hopeless that he demanded its surrender to 'the pious cause of Parliament', on pain of annihilation by his vastly superior force. Belasyse replied that he had no authority to comply with Parliament's demands. What he did not know was the extent to which the Royalist war effort had collapsed everywhere else. By this time, Charles was effectively boxed in at Oxford, his requests for an armistice to discuss terms having been flatly turned down. With characteristic cunning, he contrived to escape (disguised as a servant) from his capital with a view to surrendering to the Scots at Newark. On 5 May, in the Saracen's Head at Southwell, he formally surrendered to

Scottish Commissioners. Instructed to order the surrender of the garrison at Newark, he obeyed – thereby providing Belasyse with the authority he needed to submit to Poyntz's demands.

# The Aftermath

On 8 May 1646, Belasyse led his eighteen hundred-strong garrison out of Newark, having abandoned all artillery and muskets, although under the terms of the surrender 'gentlemen' were permitted to retain small arms. The victors could afford to be generous. Townsfolk were conscripted to demolish the painstakingly constructed defensive earthworks but, fortunately, the Roundheads did not remain to supervise the work, and so portions survived.

As for Charles, his illusions concerning the magnanimity of the Scots were soon dispelled. Travelling north with Leslie's army, he was treated not as an honoured guest, but rather as a prisoner, a close watch being kept upon him at all times. This surveillance continued at Newcastle, where his reputation for duplicity gathered momentum as he parleyed both with the Scots, who wanted him to establish Presbyterianism in England, and with Parliament, which sought to impose constitutional safeguards against monarchical excesses. He hoped to gain by exploiting the differences between England and Scotland and, within the English camp, the developing rivalry between Parliament and the New Model Army. Having negotiated the best terms they could, the Scots eventually sold Charles to Parliament for cash.

Installed at Holdenby House, near Northampton, the king enjoyed considerably more freedom of movement, including permission to visit neighbouring estates, while Parliament and the New Model Army fought over the spoils, Parliament insisting on a government without a monarch and the New Model Army, unpaid and dissatisfied, arguing for a restored Charles and a constitutionally strengthened Parliament ruling in blissful union. At length, the army resolved to consolidate its position by acquiring the Royal Person and, on 3 June 1647, the king was taken from Holdenby, via Newmarket and Hatfield to Hampton Court. The reaction at Westminster was one of outrage, although a minority, under the tutelage of Cromwell, had instigated the proceedings.

In order to resolve the situation, three preconditions were required: political unity and objectivity on behalf of Parliament, a measure of tolerance from the Presbyterians and a display of goodwill from the king – none of which was in evidence. Parliament stubbornly refused to acknowledge the role played by the army in the late conflict. With the war now over, it was something to be disbanded – preferably without pay. Moreover, the rank and file within the army suspected that the conservative Presbyterian element within Parliament had no desire to permit freedom of worship beyond its own brand of Presbyterianism. In itself, this suspicion led to deep divisions within the ranks.

In an effort to secure Charles's support, Cromwell tried to persuade him to agree to accept some measure of reform. While entering into positive discussion of Cromwell's proposals, however, the king was simultaneously trying to persuade the Scots to invade England – this time, on his behalf – at a cost of agreeing to establish Presbyterianism in England for a minimum period of three years. Realizing that, once more, he had need of Prince Rupert, he also wrote to his nephew, reminding him that he (the Prince) stood second only to the king's own children in his affections – an assertion which Rupert, despite all that had gone before, seems to have had little difficulty in accepting. When Parliament got wind of these discussions, Charles fled to the Isle of Wight – having succeeded, by his actions, in reuniting the army and sealing his own fate.

# *The Walk*

**Distance:**   3 miles (5 km)

The starting point for the walk is the Tourist Office in Castle Gate (point A), in front of Newark Castle itself (Pathfinder 796 797540). This is called the Gilstrap Centre. It is open daily (including Sundays) and it makes a useful starting point because maps and information sheets can be obtained there.

Emerging from the centre, turn left into Castle Gate and walk straight ahead, over Bargate and into Northgate. Cross over to the other side of the road and turn to the right at the traffic lights into Queens Road. Walk on, past Kings Road, to Appletongate and turn right. At the opposite corner are the remains of The Friary, where lived, at the time of the Civil War, Lord Deincourt, a hardy Royalist. According to local tradition, hoards of money and valuables were hidden in vaults for safety – where they remain. From time to time, figures of hooded monks are reputedly seen, perhaps guarding the treasure, which waits to be reclaimed.

Continue along Appletongate and Newark Museum is on the left. Containing some interesting items from the Civil War, it can be visited most afternoons (except Thursdays) from 2.00 p.m. to 5.00 p.m. After visiting

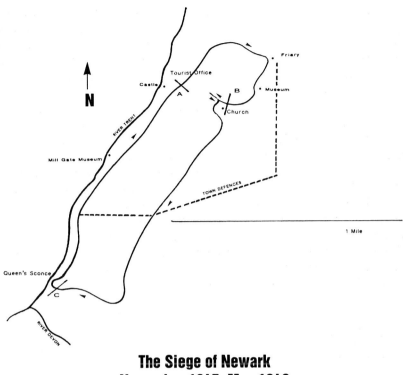

**N**

## The Siege of Newark
## November 1645–May 1646

the museum, cross the road and, slightly to the right is Mount Lane. Looking up at St Mary's church (Pathfinder 796 799539) (point B) from Mount Lane, one can see a hole in the spire, supposedly the result of a Roundhead cannon shot. When they entered the town, the Roundheads destroyed the font, a fact attested to on a nearby pillar. A plaque in the churchyard commemorates several Royalist officers, killed in various actions during the siege, and whose bodies were removed from the church crypt for reburial in 1883.

Opposite the church is Kirkgate. Walk a little way down here and on the right, there will be seen a half-timbered house, entitled Charles I Coffee House, although popularly known as Queen Henrietta Maria's House. While in Newark, the queen stayed here, in the home of Colonel Charles Leeke. It is reputedly haunted.

Walk back towards the church and across to the Market Place. At the far right-hand corner is the National Westminster Bank, bearing a plaque stating that a house belonging to the Mayor of Newark during the Civil War, Hercules Clay, once stood on the site. One night during the siege, Clay

Newark Castle from the Mill Lane Bridge, which spans the River Trent

dreamed that his house had been destroyed in a bombardment (which was more or less continuous, day and night). The following night, he had the same dream. When it occurred for the third night in succession, he took it as an omen and moved out. Shortly after, the house took a direct hit. In his will, among other charitable bequests, Clay left £100 to the vicar of St Mary's on condition that he preach a sermon on 11 March every year, as a form of thanksgiving for his divine deliverance from destruction.

Opposite the bank is another half-timbered house, the Governors' House, where the Governors of Newark – Sir John Henderson, Sir Richard Byron, Richard Willys and Lord Belasyse – resided. Prince Rupert spent some time here during his argument with the king over the surrender of Bristol. The Market Place was the scene of much mutinous behaviour by Royalist troops, most of whom supported the prince.

On the far left of the Market Place, opposite the National Westminster Bank, is the Arcade, leading through to Cartergate (a continuation of Appletongate). Walk through the Arcade, turning right on to Cartergate. Continue down Cartergate to the junction with Portland Street and Albert Street. Choose Albert Street to the left. Walk on down Albert Street and across the roundabout at Boundary Road. Just beyond St Catherines Close, on the right, is a footpath leading to Valley Prospect and Devon Park. Take this path which leads directly to the Queen's Sconce (Pathfinder 796

791531) (point C). It is remarkably well preserved and perhaps merits a little more in the way of protection than it has at present. Intended to defend the southern approaches to the town, its raised corner bastions can still be discerned. The surrounding ditch is also well defined.

Walk diagonally across the Sconce, skirting the park. Spring House public house (where refreshment can be taken) will be seen standing at the junction of Mill Gate and Victoria Street. Take the Mill Gate road to the left of the pub. Beyond the left-hand side of the road, running parallel with Mill Gate, is the River Trent. Mill Lane, off Mill Gate, runs over the river and provides a splendid view of the castle. Adjacent to Mill Lane is the Mill Gate Folk Museum complex (Pathfinder 796 795537), which also contains a café and bar (telephone (0636) 79403 for details).

Mill Gate leads on to Castle Gate and the Tourist Office, the starting pont of the walk. The castle ruins may be viewed – although ruins are all that remain of a once magnificent defensive structure. The castle was built in the early twelfth century and King John died there in 1216. It was under siege as early as 1218, following an ownership dispute. During the Civil War, it was the target of heavy fire, which it survived, only to be destroyed on Parliament's orders in 1647.

# Further Explorations

The site of a siege can often provide an exciting battlefield walk, with plenty to see for miles around. Of the villages encircling Newark, which played a part in siege operations, Hawton retains the most obvious evidence of fortification. Remains of one of three redoubts which encircled the village can be seen to the west, beside the River Devon (Pathfinder 796 785512). Although the best view is necessarily an aerial one, the ramparts may still readily be distinguished at ground level.

Rather less clearly defined remains can be discerned at Muskham Bridge (Pathfinder 796 786562). This, it will be recollected, was a Royalist fortification, captured by the besiegers. Again, the Crankley Point redoubt, constructed by the Scots to keep open a line of retreat across the Trent, can also be identified (Pathfinder 797 800560).

As well as Newark, the Royalists occupied many of the country houses in the vicinity, including Shelford Manor (Landranger 129 6743), the Royalists putting up a stout defence from the manor-house and the church tower. In both cases, they had to be burned out. The Parliamentarian reputation for wanton destruction is not wholly unwarranted, for many estates suffered in the same way. Wiverton Hall

(Landranger 129 7136), for example, was pulled down after the Royalist garrison surrendered.

At the time of the Civil War, Belvoir Castle (Landranger 130 8133), was called Belvedere and a castle had stood on the site since Norman times. The first castle had been built by Robert de Todeni, Standard Bearer to William the Conqueror. Early in the conflict, Belvoir had been seized for the king by one Gervais Lucas, a servant of the Parliamentarian owner. Prince Rupert, in disgrace after the loss of Bristol, was involved in a skirmish here in October 1645. At Belvoir Bridge, with a little over one hundred followers, he was met by the Parliamentarian Colonel Rossiter, at the head of three times that number. By a combination of daring and evasion (thanks to an intimate knowledge of the area), Rupert both outfought and outwitted Rossiter, to gain the safety of the castle. It was during his stay at Belvoir that the king placed him under house arrest – an order the prince ignored. After the war, Belvoir, in company with many buildings of note, was slighted by Parliament as a punishment for supporting the Royalists – an unfortunate decision considering the Parliamentarian sympathies of the owners. (For details of opening times of the present Belvoir House, telephone (0476) 870262.)

Nottingham, of course, is rich in Civil War associations. Although it was here that Charles raised his banner on 22 August 1642, and despite the fact that Newark, only 18 miles away was staunchly Royalist, Nottingham remained a Parliamentarian garrison throughout. By no means all the citizens were staunch Parliamentarians, however, and many rebelled against the disciplinarian governor, Colonel John Hutchinson, who declared that if the Royalists wanted to take Nottingham, they would have to wade through blood. When an attacking force of around one thousand Royalist troops managed to fight its way to the castle gates, it was beaten back and allegedly left a river of blood which froze in the January snow. Despite Nottingham's loyalty, its castle joined Belvoir in being reduced to ruins when the war ended. This fortified site, which could rightly boast participation in the wars between Danes and Saxons, the Baronial Wars and the Wars of the Roses, was levelled and the castle masonry, which had once echoed to the voices of kings, was sold as paving stones.

# Further Information

One advantage of a town-based walk is that getting there poses few problems. Situated on the Great North Road (A1), Newark is easily accessible from both north and south, while the A617 and A46 provide access from the North and South Midlands respectively.

Newark is also well serviced by British Rail, occupying a position on the King's Cross to Edinburgh line (tel: (0636) 707173 for further information). For National Express coach information, telephone (0602) 585317.

Ordnance Survey maps for the area are Landrangers 121, 129 and 130, and Pathfinders 796 (Newark East) and 797 (Newark West). A Newark street map, which can be bought in the town, should also be of value. Readily available reading is rather thin on the ground. Peter Young's *Sieges of the Great Civil War* (Bell & Hyman, 1978) contains an account of the siege, but the most valuable secondary sources emanate from Nottinghamshire County Council, which has produced a series of booklets on the Civil War in Nottinghamshire. Details of these publications may be obtained from Nottinghamshire County Council, Leisure Services (Tourism Section), Trent Bridge House, Fox Road, West Bridgford, Nottingham NG2 6BJ (tel: (0602) 823823).

# 14
# THE BATTLE OF WORCESTER
## 3 September 1651

## *The Road to Worcester*

The Civil War both began and ended at Worcester. The first engagement of any consequence took place at Powick Bridge on 23 September 1642, while the last battle, occasioned by the return of the Prince of Wales, was fought to a conclusion in the same locality. The Battle of Powick Bridge cost little more than fifty Roundhead lives, but it set a pattern for many of the early encounters between Roundheads and Cavaliers – the devil-may-care Cavalier cavalry charge, against which the opposition collapsed.

Nine years on, the seemingly invincible New Model Army had quenched the fire and brimstone of Prince Rupert's dashing individualism. The king had lost his head and the king's son, Charles Stuart, had mounted an invasion, landing in Scotland on 23 June 1650. On 3 September, at Dunbar, Charles's Scottish army, under the command of the distinguished David Leslie, was decimated by the New Model Army, led in person by Cromwell.

Notwithstanding this unqualified disaster, Charles immediately set about recruiting a new army, calling on Scots and long-suffering English Royalists, most of whom had only their lives left to give, to which the prospective monarch, like his father, was only too happy to lay claim. Cromwell having been taken seriously (some thought, fatally) ill, the royal claimant was able to amass a new task force of fourteen thousand men. Without Cromwell at the helm, the New Model Army commanders, Lambert, Monck and Harrison, seemed to flounder, and Charles II was crowned at Scone on New Year's Day, 1651.

It was not until the spring of 1651 that the Protector was sufficiently recovered to take the field once more. It is often said that he won his battles through the meticulous planning which went into each campaign, and this was never more true than in his strategy for meeting the young Charles's challenge to his power. Sensing that a decisive victory was more likely to be

Powick Bridge, the scene of the first and part of the last battles of the first Civil War. Powick is to the left, Worcester to the right, with the Malvern Hills in the background

gained on English than on Scottish soil, Cromwell withdrew his troops from the borders, leaving open an inviting route to the south.

Charles, with chiefs of staff Leslie and the Duke of Hamilton, took the bait, crossing the border to the north of Carlisle, while Cromwell cut off their supply lines and occupied Perth and Stirling. Having ensured that there was now no way back for the Royalists, the New Model Army set off in pursuit, closing in to harass the Royalist rearguard.

With his father's optimism, Charles had expected to be able to march to London unhindered, and had reached Warrington before realizing that his plans would have to be reviewed. In veering west, towards Shrewsbury, he hoped to attract much-needed support from Wales. But Shrewsbury closed its gates against him. While Lambert harassed the Royalist rear, Cromwell had taken a circuitous route towards the capital, linking up again with Lambert at Warwick, and when General Fleetwood, who had been recruiting in London, added his weight, the total strength of the New Model Army in the field reached almost thirty thousand. The Royalists, whose exposed position was now of real concern to Leslie, numbered just thirteen thousand. Indeed, the outcome of any battle can hardly have been in doubt. By gathering together such a huge army, Cromwell hoped not merely to trounce the Royalists but to crush them beyond repair.

# The Battle of Worcester

Having been rejected at Shrewsbury, the invaders moved on to Worcester, where they met with more success, the citizens giving them leave to enter on 22 August after the token Parliamentary garrison had respectfully withdrawn. The city defences having been slighted, one feels that a speedy cut and thrust movement by Cromwell would have finished matters there and then. However, his careful planning allowed the rebels a precious week in which to consolidate their position. An earthwork to the south of the city, grandly named Fort Royal, was speedily constructed and the Duke of Hamilton acquired a medieval house, The Commandery, as a military headquarters.

With Charles boxed-in at Worcester, Cromwell was in no hurry to press home his advantage. In marching up from Evesham, the New Model Army was already blocking the route to London. To cut off the avenue of retreat to the West Country, the bridge at Upton upon Severn, to the south of Worcester, was seized by Lambert on 29 August. Rejecting the possibility of a full-frontal assault from the east, against fortified positions, Cromwell decided upon an attack from the south. With thirty thousand men at his command, he could afford to take the risks attendant on dividing his force. While he cautiously approached the city from the south-east, General Fleetwood, with eleven thousand men, advanced along the west bank of the Severn. Fleetwood's progress was slow because he was towing twenty boats, with which he hoped to bridge the Teme and Severn where they joined – the Royalists having destroyed existing bridges. In addition, Fleetwood's force was subdivided for the purpose of taking Powick Bridge, held by the Royalists and where it still might be possible to effect a Teme crossing.

The Powick defenders were easily overrun, falling back towards the town. The bridging process to the east went surprisingly smoothly. The activity was easily discernible from the town and Cromwell's fear – unfounded as it turned out – was that the bridge builders would have to work under heavy fire. However, Charles seemed more impressed by the potential for counter-attack caused by the division and subdivision of the attacking army. With every available man, he abandoned his defensive positions and launched an all-out assault against the New Model Army's right wing, which gave way against the impetus of the Royalist charge. Cromwell, who had crossed the makeshift bridge and was directing operations against the Royalist contingent between the Teme and the city defences, perceived the danger and hurried back to retrieve the situation.

Charles had taken up an effective position on Red Hill, which he was not to quit until three or four hours of bitter fighting forced him to retreat into

*The Battle of Worcester* by Thomas Woodward (The Commandery, Worcester City Council)

the city. His efforts to launch a counter-attack of his own proved futile when the Scots threw down their arms and sought to save themselves. The English cavalry held firm and managed to stem the tide, however, giving Charles sufficient time to effect his escape.

The Scots were fighting on the anniversary of Dunbar, which perhaps did nothing for their self-confidence, and Leslie, out of his depth, had been more successful fighting against the underdogs, as at Newark, than with them. The Scots infantry were cut down in the city's narrow streets while the cavalry, which abandoned them to their fate, secured for themselves only a few more hours of freedom before being hunted down.

## The Aftermath

Worcester marked the end of the third and final phase of the English Civil War. Cromwell's casualties were light – no more than a few hundred killed against over two thousand Royalist dead. Additionally, ten thousand Royalist prisoners – including six hundred officers – were taken. Some senior officers, such as Leslie (captured in Yorkshire) and Lauderdale, were to suffer imprisonment until the Restoration in 1660. The less fortunate Derby was executed. Cromwell assumed the mantle of statesman and, ultimately, 'Lord Protector', leading an administration financed, in part, by heavy 'fines' levied upon defeated Royalists and Catholics.

Worcestershire has always been rich in folklore and has many associations with witchcraft and black magic, stories of which practices continue to the present day. It is, perhaps, only natural that some of these tales relate to the Battle of Worcester. For example, according to uniformed Royalist opinion, Roundhead supremacy on the field of battle was not due to superior generalship and the efficiency of the New Model Army. Far more sinister forces, it was argued at the time, were at work – a belief confirmed by events immediately prior to the confrontation. On the morning of the battle, Cromwell, accompanied by a friend, ventured into a wood near his campsite and was observed striking a bargain with an elderly personage who brandished a roll of parchment. The bartering was clearly Mephistophelean in nature and revolved around the ownership of Cromwell's soul. Although he had evidently hoped to sell it for twenty-one years of earthly success, the stranger knocked him down to a more modest seven years. The meeting left Cromwell completely confident of supremacy in the coming battle – the pledge being redeemed with his death, exactly seven years later, on 3 September 1658.

Out of Worcester also grew undeniably the most romantic legend associated with the Civil War – the escape of the richest prize of all, the heir to the throne. Much has been written concerning Charles's bravery, but he had no reservations about abandoning his beaten army to its wretched fate. Originally, Charles had intended striking out north, for Scotland, initially taking refuge at Boscobel House, near Wolverhampton. In the grounds of Boscobel occurred the famous incident of the heir and the oak. To outwit his pursuers, he hid with a friend, Colonel William Carlis, in the branches of a tall oak tree. While Roundhead search parties ran to and fro beneath him, Charles, honouring Carlis by using the latter's arm as a pillow, dozed off. The arm growing numb, Carlis had to pinch the Royal Person in order to free himself.

Although the poor country folk who sheltered him during his flight, risked their lives in so doing, Charles continued to suspect everyone. On 10 September, Parliament issued a proclamation offering a £1,000 reward for the apprehension of 'Charles Stuart, son to the late Tyrant', a fabulous fortune to many of his aiders and abetters. And yet, thanks to the loyalty of those who stood to gain nothing, he managed to complete his escape. Banter with lowly members of the public he encountered from time to time included an exchange with a village blacksmith, during which Charles remarked that if Charles Stuart was captured, he deserved to be hanged for calling in the Scots.

Second only to the oak tree incident in popularity, is the time Charles spent disguised as a servant of Jane Lane, daughter of a notable cavalier. Jane was in possession of a travel pass for two people, enabling her to visit the staunchly Royalist Norton family at Abbots Leigh, near Bristol. This represented a heaven-sent opportunity for the prince to get clear of the Midlands. However, it transpired that no sea passage could be secured at Bristol, that most Royalist of royal ports, and so it was decided that, in the company of Jane Lane, he would make for the south coast.

At Charmouth, it seemed that his luck had turned, for he did manage to secure the services of a ship. In the event, it did not appear, as arranged, and so he had little choice but to try elsewhere. While in hiding at Trent, near Sherborne, he was informed by his agents that a passage to France had been secured at Brighton, which was good news even if it did entail a hazardous 50-mile journey across country. Despite the risks, the journey was completed successfully and, on 15 October, he arrived in France to begin a nine year period of exile. Doubtless, Cromwell was secretly pleased to learn of his safe arrival. The prospect of having to contend with another captive Stuart would have been too much to bear.

# The Walk

**Distance:**     6½ miles (10½ km)

Begin at The Commandery (point A) on Sidbury (Pathfinder 996 853544). This is the building that was the Royalist headquarters during the battle. With a rich and varied history of its own which can be traced back to the early thirteenth century, it now houses Worcester's Civil War Centre, and has an impressive museum dedicated entirely to the conflict as well as much useful information about Worcester's role in the war. The Commandery is open Monday to Saturday 10.00 a.m. to 5.00 p.m. and on Sunday afternoons 1.30 p.m. to 5.30 p.m. all year.

Emerging from The Commandery, turn left and take the next turning on the left into Wylds Lane (in 1651, The Commandery belonged to the Wylde family, who were wealthy Royalist merchants). Across the road, to the right, Fort Royal Park is visible. The park constitutes the remains of the earthwork, constructed by the Royalists as a defence against attack from the south. It was from Fort Royal that Charles launched his assault on Red Hill.

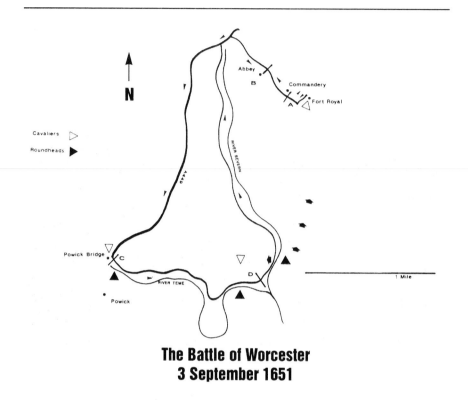

## The Battle of Worcester
## 3 September 1651

Now walk back past The Commandery and straight up into College Street, to Worcester Cathedral (point B). Much internal damage was wrought in 1642 by Roundhead troops, against whom are levied the usual charges of using the nave to stable horses. No problems should be experienced in gaining entry to the cathedral. However, although entry fees are not levied, a prominent notice at the entrance announces that visitors are expected to leave a donation of at least £1.50.

From the cathedral, turn left and continue straight up to Deansway, turning sharp left at the top into Bridge Street, and so over the River Severn. At the roundabout, beyond the cricket ground, turn left down Bromwich Road (the A449). After about 1 mile, at a roundabout, this road becomes Malvern Road and leads to Powick Bridge. A little way along, on the right, the old road to the original Powick Bridge branches off. Take this turning, to follow the route taken by the Royalists who were commissioned to hold the bridge. Rounding a bend in this road, the old bridge comes into view, as do the Malvern Hills. The old bridge stands to the left of the modern bridge and the village, maintaining a discreet distance from an expanding Worcester, seems content to remain in the shadow of its neighbour. Walk past the old factory (actually the site of what was the first hydro-electric

Looking towards Worcester from the confluence of the Teme and the Severn, where the Roundheads effected a crossing of both rivers

power station in the country) and on to the bridge (Pathfinder 996 835525) (point C). One may wish to walk over the bridge and on into Powick, to examine the marks where musket shot damaged the stone work, and to take refreshment at the Vernon Arms.

If the latter course has been taken, return to the bridge and on the Worcester side, take the riverside path, leading back to Worcester. The path, alongside the Teme, is well defined, and is punctuated with well-maintained stiles. Follow the path for about half a mile. An arrow, roughly painted in red, on what was once an old gatepost, directs one to the left. This saves following the course of the river while it meanders circuitously southwards. Eventually, the junction with the Severn is reached (Pathfinder 996 850522) (point D). At this point, the Roundhead bridge of boats spanned the Teme, to the south, and the Severn, to the east. Both stretches of river appear to be narrow, although they would doubtless have been wider three hundred years ago.

The landscape is still quite open and not too much changed from that experienced by the combatants. The Royalists occupied the land to the north of the footpath, harassing Fleetwood's men who were trying to bridge the Teme and the Severn. Once the Severn was bridged, Cromwell was able to cross over and join Fleetwood in pushing the Royalists back towards the city.

Follow the Severn back into Worcester (seats, for the convenience of walkers are placed at intervals along the river bank). As the city is approached, the path becomes paved, developing into Bromwich Parade. Having left Fleetwood to fight on alone, Cromwell recrossed the Severn and pressed on to Worcester, where he drove Charles off Red Hill and back into the city.

Bromwich Parade leads back to the bridge by the rear of the cricket ground, where one's steps can be retraced to The Commandery.

## *Further Explorations*

Worcester's role in the major armed conflicts which have afflicted the British Isles can be traced back to Anglo-Saxon times. By the late tenth century, the Danes, having more or less exhausted the pickings afforded by eastern climes, were foraging well into Cotswold country. From time to time, Worcester suffered from their raids. When these occurred, the citizens would temporarily forsake their homes for the relative safety of Bevere Island (Landranger 150 8359). On one such occasion, the elderly and infirm were caught napping and, being unable to make good their escape, were butchered by the invaders. Having satisfied their blood-lust and with their craft weighed down with booty, the Danes departed. Returning to find the settlement ablaze, the peace-loving citizens also discovered a solitary Dane, whose greed had caused him, quite literally, to miss the boat. He was caught trying to remove the cathedral's Sanctus Bell. Flayed alive, his skin was tanned and for many years afterwards it adorned the west door of the cathedral.

Three miles to the west of Worcester lies Spetchley Park (Landranger 150 8953), the home of the Berkeley family for over three hundred years. Robert Berkeley was one of those who supported Charles I in the ship money controversy and, as a judge, decided against Hampden for his refusal to pay the unpopular tax. In due course, Berkeley found himself on trial for his actions. Deprived of his office, he was imprisoned in the Tower and fined the enormous sum of £20,000. His home was used by Roundhead troops, but it was the Royalists who burned it to the ground. When Berkeley managed to raise half of his fine, he was released from the Tower to find his home destroyed. Only the stables were left standing, and it was here that he himself lived for the remaining five years of his life.

The only settlement of any size in the vicinity of Worcester is Droitwich (Landranger 150 8963). It played little part in the conflict although it served as a useful outpost from which sorties aimed at destroying Parliamentary garrisons based in outlying manor-houses could be organized. Many country seats of established West Midlands families suffered destruction as a result.

Reference has already been made to the supreme sacrifice of Oxford University in donating its fine old plate to be melted down in the royal cause. In early September 1642, the baggage train comprising this exceedingly precious cargo was to be found trundling laboriously up the Severn Valley, en route to the king at Shrewsbury. Considering its value, the cargo was poorly guarded by a small detachment under the command of Sir John Byron, and Essex dispatched Captain Nathaniel Fiennes with a body of cavalry to intercept it. Fortunately for Byron – and the Royalist treasure – Prince Rupert had decided to see him safely home and had left Shrewsbury for this purpose.

The train crawled into Worcester, in relative safety, on 16 September, and when Rupert reached the city, volunteers brought his strength up to around one thousand men – roughly equal, but certainly not numerically superior, to Fiennes' command. Learning that the Roundheads were close at hand, the prince ordered Byron to strike camp while he and his cavaliers rode out to scout the Powick Bridge locality, where Roundhead horsemen had been reported. As none were in sight, the Royalists dismounted and relaxed in the field approaching the old bridge.

As they lay basking in the late summer sunshine, Fiennes came into view, galloping over the bridge towards them. Mounting hurriedly, Rupert led his men in the first of his furious charges, catching the Roundheads on the hop. Retreating in confusion, Fiennes' vanguard was pressing against the main body of horse still advancing up the narrow lane leading from the bridge. About fifty Roundheads were killed – some of these trying to cross the river – and as many again taken prisoner. All the senior Royalists, except Rupert, were wounded.

Undoubtedly, this first battle at Powick Bridge was a Royalist success, establishing Rupert's reputation as a fearless commander. The convoy plodded on to reach its destination intact – to discover that the Oxford plate was not of sufficiently high quality for melting down and recycling as coinage. Essex occupied Worcester on the day after the fight and this fact was used to good effect in the propaganda war, with Parliamentarian claims to the effect that Fiennes had won a 'famous victory', leading to a panic-stricken Royalist evacuation of the city. Although special services of thanksgiving were ordered throughout the country, Parliament was worried. Fiennes had managed to rally some of his men and force a counter-attack, but even this had withered against the impetus of Rupert's onslaught, and Essex embarked on a review of his training programme.

As for Worcester, it was only temporarily under Roundhead control. Curiously enough, Parliament seems to have attached little value to it and appeared happy for the city to remain a Royalist stronghold throughout the conflict.

# *Further Information*

By road, Worcester is reached by taking the junction 7 exit from the M5. An effective one-way system in the town centre keeps traffic on the move, although local traffic travels at an alarming pace. The tendency is to get off the road at the first available opportunity. I use the car-park off Newport Street by the bridge. If shopping is not included in the itinerary, the best day to visit is Sunday, when parking is no problem and room can be found on the short-stay car-park opposite The Commandery.

Worcester has two railway stations, Shrub Hill station, connecting the city with London Paddington (tel: 0452 529501), and the Foregate Street connection with Birmingham (tel: 021 643 2711). There is a direct National Express coach link between London and Worcester, telephone 021 622 4373 for details.

The Tourist Office is situated in The Guildhall in the High Street. It is advisable to telephone before visiting on (0905) 726311.

Ordnance Survey maps for the area are Landranger 150 and Pathfinder 996. Further reading is provided by Roy Sherwood in *The Civil War in the Midlands 1642–51* (second edition, Alan Sutton Publishing, 1992) and Richard Ollard in *The Escape of Charles II* (Hodder & Stoughton, 1966).

PART FOUR: THE TWENTIETH CENTURY

# INTRODUCTION

The Midlands is an area rich in Second World War airfields. On the old 1 inch Ordnance Survey maps, they were depicted in their full glory. The metric series depicts airfields with greatly reduced features, mirroring the changes in land use. In present-day terms, the requirements of the developer have wreaked havoc with what remained, although such was the scale of the expansion of airfields during the war years – over five hundred were constructed between 1939 and 1945 – that much has survived that will be of interest to the military historian. Whether this will still be the case in ten years' time is another matter and there is urgent need of a coordinated project to catalogue that which has survived, with a view to its preservation.

Second World War airfields usually had three intersecting runways, the USAAF bomber fields comprising a main runway of around 6,000 ft in length, with two smaller runways of approximately 4,000 ft. Each field had up to five hangars of varying types, although established airfields such as Sywell (Northamptonshire) would have several more. Distributed far and wide were the various support sites – administrative, sick quarters, mess sites, sewage disposal sites and so on. By far the most distinctive, and perhaps the best loved, airfield feature was the watch-tower.

Watch-towers came in a variety of shapes and sizes. In the early days of flying, they were used as check-in points. With the development of radio, they assumed a more significant role, becoming (as the Americans called them) 'control' towers. Comparatively few survive.

After the war, while some airfields were retained, most fell into disuse. Ten years on, several were pressed back into service in a new war, the Cold War, which is itself now part of history. Where Flying Fortresses had once stood, new concrete structures housing missiles were sited. Ultimately, these, too, were abandoned. Only the launching pads remain as evidence of this reprieve from dereliction. But it is in the very decay that the attraction of Second World War airfields is to be found. Look and explore before it is too late, for they will soon be gone forever.

# 15
# POLEBROOK AIRFIELD
## 1941–5

## *The Road to Polebrook*

An interesting facet of battlefields is the military significance many locations have retained through the centuries. For example, Edgcote, site of a Yorkist –Lancastrian battle in 1469, had hosted a fight between Anglo-Saxons and Danes six hundred years before. Two hundred years afterwards, Charles I chose Edgcote as his base before and after Edgehill – itself the site of a present-day Ordnance Depot. The latter, of course, is out of bounds, but there remain many twentieth-century battlegrounds in the British Isles which are open to the public.

With the declaration of war in 1939, the Midlands once more assumed the strategic significance for which it has been valued throughout the centuries. In some haste, the East Anglian-based bomber squadrons abandoned their bases to retreat inland, hopefully out of range of the *Luftwaffe*. However, in addition to maintaining existing stocks of aircraft to meet operational demand, the factories had to cope with the insatiable appetite of the developing Operational Training Units.

The landscape was transformed as pastures became concrete runways, over which rumbled mighty Blenheims and Wellingtons. Vulnerable in the air, the bombers were sitting ducks when immobile on the ground and the increasing incidence of Junker attacks rendered it necessary to disperse them to 'satellite' stations wherever possible – the latter being constructed to service the main operational fields.

During the early years of the war, demand for trained crews and machines far outstripped supply, forcing the satellite stations to assume a more prominent role. Training units took on the job of 'nickelling' – making sorties over enemy territory to drop propaganda leaflets. (In due course, bombs were also added to the cargo.) But there was a limit to the extent of operation work the training units could undertake and the shortage of trained crews grew more acute. Clearly, if Operational Training Units could not concentrate on training crews, then the shortfall in trained crews would never be made up.

Indeed, the nature of training itself was constantly assuming new dimensions – overseas delivery of aircraft, the specialist schooling involved in training reconnaissance pilots and, not least, the need to train glider pilots for prospective airborne operations. In all, the system was stretched to its limits and the future looked bleak until 1942 when three things happened.

The first event was the arrival of the Lancaster bomber. Heavily armed and with four engines, it survived the war years to take on a new lease of life as a passenger airliner. And, what was more important for the trained manpower shortage, it required only one pilot.

The second event was the arrival at Bomber Command of Arthur Harris, whose belief in commitment to total war in the air did much to revitalize flagging morale.

The third momentous event of 1942 – and probably the most momentous of the three – was the arrival *en masse* of American air crews in the spring. America's entry to the war in December 1941 did, it is true, have a negative aspect, disrupting Lend-Lease arrangements as America herself was now in need of materials and machines, including heavy bombers. However, on the very day Harris was appointed Commander-in-Chief of Bomber Command, American Bomber Command in England was established at High Wycombe. The Yanks were coming – and in the role of senior partners.

# Polebrook Airfield

Work on Polebrook Airfield began in late 1940. The airfield began life as a satellite field, opening for business in its own right on 26 May 1941. Embryonic Flying Fortresses arrived in June – well before the Americans, who suggested that the RAF should use them for training purposes only until such teething troubles as existed were ironed out. Against this advice, but to help ease the aircraft shortage, the Fortresses were immediately pressed into service. Attacks on occupied European targets failed and 90 Squadron, formed to fly the new Fortresses, was disbanded.

When the Americans did come, they arrived in style and in bulk – almost one thousand officers and men, with thirty-eight Fortresses being shared between Polebrook and Grafton Underwood. Crews of 97 Bombing Group began with diversionary missions, none too glamorous a role but essential for taking the pressure off squadrons bound for the real target. Bombing missions to occupied France followed soon after, continuing until

A B–17C Fortress 1 of 90 Squadron coming in to land at Polebrook in 1941, with construction work still in progress (Imperial War Museum)

November 1942 when the Fortresses were moved to North Africa to consolidate the Allied position following Montgomery's success at Alamein.

During 1942, work began on upgrading Polebrook, and on lengthening the runways for the accommodation of no less than four B-17 squadrons of 351 Bombing Group, which were to strike deep into the heart of Germany at railway yards, submarine bases and V-Rocket launching sites. Perhaps the most celebrated member of 351 Squadron was the film star Clark Gable, who flew on several daylight raids. In the guise of gunner, he acquired some stirring film footage (16,000 ft of 16 mm film), which was to be used by Warner Brothers in feature films geared towards the war effort. Another, as yet unknown, visitor to Polebrook was Major Paul Tibbets, who was to pilot the *Enola Gay* to Hiroshima with the first atomic bomb on board.

Inevitably, there were losses, with some B-17s destined never to return to base. Of course, all losses were occasions for sadness, but the circumstances surrounding some were positively heart-breaking. Early in 1944, a crippled B-17 with casualties on board was being piloted back to Polebrook by the navigator and gunner. On trying to land at the third attempt, they crashed and everyone on board was killed. Another incident occurred in November 1943, when a number of captured enemy aircraft were being flown to Polebrook for training purposes. A Junker and a Heinkel landed at opposite ends of the same runway and, in efforts to avoid a collision, the Heinkel pilot crashed in flames. One of the most difficult tasks a commanding officer would have to undertake was informing next-of-kin that a husband or son had been killed after returning from a mission, or had lost a life on non-combatant operations. As the years wore on and Germany's capability in the air dwindled, the need for such letters thankfully became markedly less frequent.

# The Aftermath

The last operation undertaken at Polebrook by 351 Bombing Group during the Second World War took place on 25 April 1945. Three months later, by 10 July, the last of the B-17s had gone home, and the field was returned to the RAF Maintenance Command to be used largely for aircraft storage purposes. Ultimately, it assumed the role for which it was originally intended, as a satellite field for RAF Upwood, before being taken out of

Attempts to reduce the risk of enemy attacks on airfields included the camouflaging of grounded bombers. This photograph shows an American B–17 in the process of being covered with camouflage netting at Polebrook in 1943 (US Air Force)

service in October 1948.

Along with hundreds of other wartime airfields, Polebrook literally went to seed. Perimeter paths sprouted grass and the only fliers to home in on the watch-tower were nesting starlings. This state of affairs lasted for ten years, until the decision was made for Polebrook to play a part in another war. This conflict had developed shortly after the conclusion of the Second World War and was known as the Cold War.

Born of distrust between the Western powers and Eastern Europe, the Cold War was fundamentally a trial of strength between the United States and the Soviet Union. While successive American presidents tried to check Soviet expansion by offering economic incentives to nations open to persuasion by either side, Russia, having no money to give away, preferred the more direct method of military occupation. Sadly, Britain also began to develop her own nuclear deterrent in the form of Polaris and Blue Streak missiles. Expenditure would be in terms of hundreds of millions of pounds and, even then, nothing could be done without American technical assistance. Therefore, an agreement was reached on the deployment of American Thor missiles.

Carefully chosen sites for the new missiles included two Northampton-shire wartime airfields, Harrington and Polebrook. Towards the end of 1959, Thor Missile Squadron 130 moved in to Polebrook along with three missile launch pads. Not unnaturally, the British wanted control over the Thor missile bases, but they also wanted Thor because its warhead was suitable for use in the development of Blue Streak. What the Americans had not told them was that, by the time Thor was installed on British sites, it was rapidly approaching obsolescence and that, in due course, it would be going out of production.

It soon became apparent that the British government was floundering. Polaris was not a land-based missile. For it to be deployed at sea, it would be necessary to build at least half-a-dozen submarines. The future of Thor was in doubt, while Blue Streak would require both investment and, more important, know-how, in which the British nuclear missile industry was glaringly lacking. In the end, the only practical choice was Polaris. A case was made out for it in terms of mobility and invulnerability, while presenting it as the natural choice for a country with a strong naval tradition. Britain's contribution to the NATO defence effort, it was argued, would be best served by the development of Polaris.

And so, on 23 August 1963, Thor Missile Squadron 130 disbanded and Polebrook was once more abandoned to nature. Four years later, the land was sold back to the Rothschilds, from whom it had been purchased almost thirty years earlier.

# *The Walk*

**Distance:**  8 miles (13 km)

The starting point for the walk is the memorial at Polebrook Airfield itself ((Pathfinder 939 101868). The entrance to the memorial site also serves as a parking area.

The USAAF 8th Air Force veterans hold their old stamping-grounds in high esteem and most of their airfields have a granite monument *in situ*. The triangular structure at Polebrook is one of the grandest, and its inscription reminds visitors that between 1943 and 1945, Flying Fortresses engaged in 311 bombing missions, sustaining losses of 175 aircraft and crews.

From the monument (point A) turn around and leave the field at the point of entry, turning left. Walk back up to the crossroads, keeping a sharp

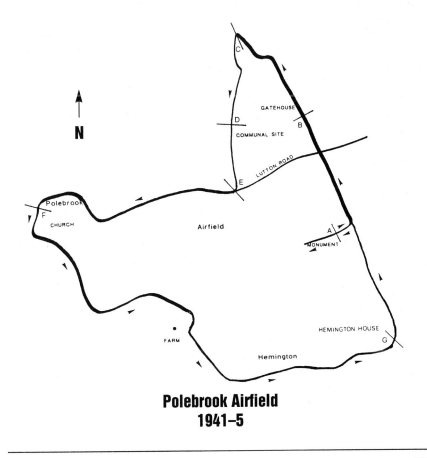

**Polebrook Airfield**
**1941–5**

look-out for remnants of old airfield architecture. Go straight on at the crossroads. On the left is the Ashton Wold estate. Eventually, again on the left, the estate entrance comes into view at the corner of which is the old thatched gatehouse (Pathfinder 939 096898) (point B). During the summer months, its rather stark appearance is softened by flowering trees and shrubbery. Innocuous as it might seem today, in October 1952 this residence was the scene of Northamptonshire's most infamous murder mystery when the estate gamekeeper, George Peach, and his wife, Lillian, were battered to death with a coal hammer. There was no evidence of burglary and the sheer ferocity of the attack suggested a revenge motive. (Lillian Peach was wearing metal hair-curlers which were driven into her skull.) Although Scotland Yard identified a clutch of suspects, no charges were ever brought. Midway through the police enquiry, either through fear or community spirit, the local villagers ceased to cooperate and the mystery remains unsolved.

Press on along the road to the next crossroads (point C). Take a left turn down the clearly-marked bridle-path. In wet weather, farm vehicles turn this into a quagmire, but horse-riders and walkers have beaten an auxiliary path through the undergrowth on the left. As one approaches the point at which one's path crosses with the estate road leading from the gatehouse (point D), one comes upon a small treasure trove of original airfield architecture. Beneath the water-tower on your left are the remains of Site No. 5, Communal Site No. 2, comprising precious few dilapidated huts. Wartime airfields amounted to far more than a length of runway with a couple of adjacent aircraft hangars. Self-supporting communities with hundreds of service personnel, they spanned a vast acreage, with several sites dispersed throughout the surrounding countryside.

As one crosses the estate road, the path veers slightly to the left, leading on through the wood, eventually bringing one out on the Polebrook to Lutton road (point E). Turn right and follow the road into Polebrook. The grass verges are wide, quite even and make for safe walking. Polebrook is an immaculate village with scarcely a blade of grass out of place. The architecture suggests the arrival of many newcomers has broken down the traditional insularity of a closed village community.

Beyond the market cross is the Red Lion, where refreshments may be taken. Otherwise, take a left turn into Church Row to see the Norman church of All Saints (Pathfinder 939 068871) (point F). If closed, there is usually a list of keyholders posted on the door. The church is very small and perhaps rather plain, although, as it maintains links with USAAF Polebrook veterans, it does have several plaques decorating the walls. One photograph depicts a Flying Fortress over the wartime airfield.

Leaving the church, turn left on to Hemington Road. Check the time by the church clock (it has only one hand which tells the hour). As one walks

The USAAF memorial at Polebrook Airfield, set against the outline of the hangars which once housed flying fortresses

out of Polebrook, there is a public footpath sign to Hemington. The path, however, has long been incorporated into a ploughed field, as indicated on OS sheet 152, and the resulting mud renders it impassable. In any event, the road itself is quiet and provides relief from the trek through Ashton Wold.

The road leads to Kingsthorpe Lodge with a host of farm buildings, on the right. Before clearing the complex, on the left you can see a gap in the hedgerow. Looking across the fields, slightly uphill, one can see a concrete structure surrounded by barbed wire. This marks the course of the main runway.

Continue walking to Hemington. On entering the village, take the road to the left, which will take one through the village and on to Hemington House (Pathfinder 939 107859) (Point G), where the road veers sharply to the left, leading back up to the airfield entrance and the starting point.

Keeping to the tarmac, walk on past the monument. To the right are the original aircraft hangars (Pathfinder 939 095869). The hangars are of two types. The one with the rounded roof is a Type J hangar, 350 ft in length and 150 ft wide. Hangars of this variety were constructed in the early years of the war, to be superseded by the Type T2 hangar – which can be seen here, alongside the Type J. The T2, with a sloping roof, is smaller and prefabricated for easy erection. Fortunately, both the J and the T2 provide excellent storage facilities, and herein lies the secret of their survival.

To the left are what one might take to be the remains of wartime concrete structures, but a closer examination reveals that these are the virtually indestructible reminders of Polebrook's Thor missile days.

Returning to the monument, one may sign the visitors' book, kept in a glass case thankfully free from the effects of vandalism.

# *Further Explorations*

This north-east corner of Northamptonshire is rich not only in its associations with the Second World War but also for its links with other conflicts at other times. On the other side of the A605, to the north of Oundle, is Fotheringhay (Landranger 141 0693). Fotheringhay Castle was the birthplace of Richard III. All that remains of the castle is a grassy mound, a place of pilgrimage for Richard's present-day adherents. It was built in the twelfth century by the first Earl of Huntingdon and extended in the fourteenth century during the reign of Edward III, after which it became a Yorkist stronghold. In 1462 Edward IV brought to Fotheringhay the remains of his father, Richard, Duke of York, and brother, Edmund, Earl of Rutland, who had met their deaths at Wakefield two years earlier. In 1587 Mary Queen of Scots was beheaded here. Upon his accession to the throne, Mary's son, James I, had the castle pulled down. It is said that a staircase was moved, intact, to the Talbot Inn at Oundle, leading to the appearance on many occasions of Mary's ghost.

Two miles to the south-west of Polebrook is Barnwell (Landranger 141 0584). Barnwell Castle dates from the Baronial Wars and was begun around 1266 by the Le Moine family who were fervent Royalists. Subsequently, ownership passed to Ramsay Abbey and then, via Sir Edward Montague, to the present owner, the Duke of Gloucester. None of the interior buildings have survived, only the 12 ft thick outer walls remaining as indicators of its youthful virility. There is a turgid local legend concerning the Le Moine family. While Baron Le Moine was away fighting in the Crusades, his two sons, Berengarius and Wintner, quarrelled over a girl. Their disagreement developed into a feud and Berengarius planned to dispose of his brother by incarcerating him in a secret room which he had specially built for the purpose. According to the story, the baron returned in the nick of time to prevent the dastardly deed, Wintner married the girl and Berengarius got his just deserts.

Stories of people being locked away in secret rooms are quite common. It will be remembered that Lord Lovel ended his days in this manner (see p. 70). A similar story, also concerning the Lovel family, is attributed to Titchmarsh Castle. Titchmarsh lies 4 miles to the south of Barnwell (Landranger 141 0279), and only a dry ditch remains to suggest that a fortification once occupied the site. In the 1830s a song entitled 'The Mistletoe Bough' was penned by T.H. Bailey and Sir Henry Bishop. It recounted the tale of 'The Mistletoe Bough Bride' – one Maude de Sydenham, daughter of William de Sydenham, the builder of Titchmarsh Castle. After William's death, Maude was married off to Sir John Lovel (of Minster Lovell). During the wedding festivities, a game of hide and seek took place, the young bride choosing to hide in a chest in a secret room. Unfortunately, she was unable to free herself from the chest and Lovel, being unfamiliar with the castle layout, was unable to find her. It was presumed that the game had been a ruse to enable her to elope with a rival lover. Centuries later, a maid stumbled upon the secret room and the chest. Raising the lid, she found a skeleton in a tattered silk wedding gown.

# Further Information

Polebrook Airfield is to be found off the A605 Oundle to Peterborough road and lies 4 miles from the Ashton and Polebrook turn-off at the roundabout introducing the Oundle by-pass. For the cost of an extra mile, it may also be approached from the Norman Cross turn-off on the A1, via Folksworth and Lutton. The Polebrook to Lutton road is crossed at the corner of Ashton Wold by a minor road leading north-westward to Tansor and Warmington and, in the opposite direction, to Polebrook Airfield, which is signposted quite prominently.

Gone, alas, are the days when Oundle boasted its own railway station. The nearest rail link is now Peterborough via the North East Inter-City line out of King's Cross (enquiries to Peterborough, (0733) 68181). For details of National Express coach services, telephone (0733) 237141. For bus services between Peterborough and Oundle, telephone United Counties on (0536) 512411.

For the Polebrook Airfield walk, refer to Ordnance Survey Landranger 142 and Pathfinder 939. To visit the places of interest described in the Further Explorations section, Landranger 141 is necessary.

Essential reading for anyone who wishes to take the subject further are two volumes in Patrick Stephens' *Action Station* series: *Action Stations 2:*

*Military Airfields of Lincolnshire and the East Midlands* by Bruce Barrymore Halpenny (Patrick Stephens, 1981) and *Action Stations 6: Military Airfields of the Cotswolds and the Central Midlands* by Michael Bowyer (Patrick Stephens, 1983). All Saints' church at Polebrook is featured in Arthur Mee's *King's England: Northamptonshire*. Bruce Barrymore Halpenny has also published four splendid collections of ghost stories connected with airfields under the titles of *Ghost Stations* (Casdec Publishing).

# FURTHER READING

Place of publication given only if outside London.

For general background reading, one need look no further than Churchill's *A History of The English-Speaking Peoples*:

Churchill, Winston S., *A History of the English-Speaking Peoples: The Birth of Britain*, Cassell & Co Ltd, 1956.
Churchill, Winston S., *A History of the English-Speaking Peoples: The New World*, Cassell & Co Ltd, 1956.

For reading relating to the Wars of the Roses, the following are recommended:

Chrimes, S.B., *Lancastrians, Yorkists and Henry VII*, Macmillan & Co Ltd, 1964.
Lander, J.R., *The Wars of the Roses*, revised edition, Alan Sutton Publishing, Stroud, 1990.
Ross, Charles, *The Wars of the Roses: A Concise History*, Thames & Hudson, 1976.

For reading relating to the English Civil War, the following are recommended:

Ashley, M., *The English Civil War*, revised edition, Alan Sutton Publishing, Stroud, 1990.
Downing, T. and Millman, M., *Civil War*, Collins & Brown Ltd, 1991.
Kenyon, John, *The Civil Wars of England*, Weidenfeld & Nicolson, 1988.

For accounts of British battles, see:

Burne, Alfred H., *The Battlefields of England*, Methuen & Co Ltd, 1950.
Burne, Alfred H., *More Battlefields of England*, Methuen & Co Ltd, 1952.
Green, Howard, *Guide to the Battlefields of Britain and Ireland*, Constable & Co Ltd, 1973.
Kinross, John, *The Battlefields of Britain*, David & Charles, Newton Abbot, 1979.

Seymour, William, *Battles in Britain 1066–1547*, Sidgwick & Jackson, 1975.

Seymour, William, *Battles in Britain 1642–1746*, Sidgwick & Jackson, 1975.

Smurthwaite, David, *The Complete Guide to the Battlefields of Britain*, Michael Joseph Ltd, 1993.

Warner, David, *British Battlefields: The South*, Osprey Publishing, 1972.

Warner, David, *British Battlefields: The Midlands*, Osprey Publishing, 1972.

Woolrych, Austin, *Battles of the English Civil War*, Batsford, 1961.


For more detailed reading, the following are recommended:


Adair, John, *John Hampden, The Patriot*, MacDonald & Jayne's, 1976.

Ashley, Maurice, *The Battle of Naseby*, Alan Sutton Publishing, Stroud, 1992.

Bennett, Michael, *The Battle of Bosworth*, Alan Sutton Publishing, Stroud, 1987.

Bennett, Michael, *Lambert Simnel and The Battle of Stoke*, Alan Sutton Publishing, Stroud, 1987.

Bowyer, Michael J., *Action Stations: Military Airfields of the Cotswolds and the Central Midlands*, Patrick Stephens, Cambridge, 1983.

Cox, D.C., *The Battle of Evesham*, Vale of Evesham Historical Society, Evesham, 1988.

Hammond, P.W., *The Battles of Barnet and Tewkesbury*, Alan Sutton Publishing, Stroud, 1993.

Kendall, Paul Murray, *Richard III*, Allen & Unwin, 1955.

Labarge, Margaret, *Simon de Montfort*, Eyre & Spottiswood, 1962.

Ollard, Richard, *The Escape of Charles II*, Hodder & Stoughton, 1966.

Priestley, E.J., *The Battle of Shrewsbury*, Shrewsbury & Atcham Borough Council, Shrewsbury, 1979.

Sherwood, Roy, *The Civil War in the Midlands 1642–51*, second edition, Alan Sutton Publishing, Stroud, 1992.

Toynbee, Margaret & Young, Peter, *Cropredy Bridge 1644: The Campaign and The Battle*, Roundwood Press, Kineton, 1977.

Warner, Tim, *Newark: Civil War and Siegeworks*, Nottinghamshire County Council, Nottingham, 1972.

Young, Peter, *Edgehill, 1642: The Campaign and The Battle*, Roundwood Press, Kineton, 1967.

——, *Naseby, 1645: The Campaign and The Battle*, Century Publishing, 1985.

——, *Sieges of the Great Civil War*, Bell & Hyman, 1978.

# INDEX OF PLACES

# INDEX OF PERSONS

Scrope, John, Lord 68
Scrope, Thomas, Lord 68
Shrewsbury, Earl of (George Talbot) 48, 57, 61
Simnel, Lambert 67, 68, 70, 71
Simons, Richard 67, 71
Sitwell, Edith 35
Skippon, Sgt-Major General Sir Philip 35, 123, 124
Smith, John 84
Somerset, 4th Duke of (Edmund Beaufort) 46, 47, 48, 49, 51, 53
Stafford, Earl of 18
Stamford, Earl of (Henry Grey) 91
Stanley, Sir Thomas, Lord 56, 57, 58, 59, 60
Stanley, Sir William 57, 60, 63
Stapleton, Sir Philip 84, 93, 94
Strafford, Earl of (Thomas Wentworth) 28, 132
Strange, Lord (George Stanley) 56, 59, 68, 69, 70
Stuart, Charles, Prince of Wales (afterwards Charles II, King of England) 21, 84, 132, 146, 147, 148, 149, 150, 151, 154
Stuart, James, Duke of York 84
Surrey, Thomas, Earl of 57
Sydenham, Maud de 167
Sydenham, William de 167

Thomas, Rhys ap 56
Thurloe, John 80
Tibbets, Paul 160
Todeni, Robert de 144
Tyler, Wat 24

Urry, Colonel 92, 94

Vermuyden, Colonel 102, 103
Verney, Sir Edmund 84, 85

Waller, Sir William 111, 112, 113, 114, 115, 116, 117, 118
Warwick, Edward, Earl of 61, 67, 68
Warwick, Earl of (Richard Neville) 27, 28, 30, 31, 37, 38, 40, 41, 46, 50, 132
Washington, John 35
Washington, Lawrence 35
Welles, Lord 37, 38, 40, 49
Welles, Sir Robert 37, 38, 39, 40, 41
Wenlock, Lord 47, 48
Whalley, Colonel 21
Widdrington, Sir William 102, 103, 104, 106
William I (King of England) 1, 8, 144
Willoughby, Lord William of Parham 101, 105
Willys, Sir Richard 137, 138, 142
Wilmot, Henry, Lord 83, 88
Woodville, Elizabeth (Queen of Edward IV) 26, 35, 61
Woodville, Sir John 30
Worcester, Thomas, Earl of 14, 16
Worcester, Earl of (John Tiptoft) 41

York, Edmund, Duke of 23
York, Richard, Duke of 24, 26, 166
York, Richard, Duke of (younger son of Edward IV) 55
Young, Arthur 84

Zouche, Lord 57